Practical Pottery and Ceramics

PRACTICAL

Pottery and Ceramics

KENNETH CLARK

A Studio Book · The Viking Press · New York

ACKNOWLEDGEMENTS

I must first, as an ex-student, say how much I owe to Miss Dora Billington for her teaching and instruction on which I have unashamedly drawn, and to my wife for her endless patience, and for her help in carrying out most of the black and white drawings. My thanks are particularly due to Mr Michael Pattrick, Principal of the Central School, for permission to use many illustrations of students' work, and to Gilbert Harding-Green, Head of the Ceramic Department, for his help and co-operation.
I am most grateful to Gordon Baldwin, Alan Caiger-Smith and Kenneth Shaw who so kindly read the script and made many constructive suggestions and comments.
I must also thank the many people whose works have helped to illustrate this book and the British Museum for permission to use illustrations from its collection.

REPRINTED 1965, 1966, 1968
FIRST PUBLISHED IN PAPERBACK 1972
PUBLISHED IN GREAT BRITAIN BY STUDIO VISTA PUBLISHERS
BLUE STAR HOUSE, HIGHGATE HILL, LONDON N19
AND IN THE USA BY THE VIKING PRESS, INC.
625 MADISON AVENUE, NEW YORK, N.Y. 10022
LIBRARY OF CONGRESS CATALOG CARD NUMBER 64-12382

SET IN 11 ON 13PT PLANTIN
PRINTED PHOTOLITHO IN GREAT BRITAIN BY J. W. ARROWSMITH LTD. BRISTOL

UK ISBN 0 289 27656 X (HARDBOUND)
    ISBN 0 289 70304 2 (PAPERBOUND)
USA SBN 670-57111-3 (HARDBOUND)
    SBN 670-02024-9 (PAPERBOUND)

Contents

Bibliography

Including books on art and design in a wide sense

Foundations of Modern Art by Ozenfant
Dover Publications, New York

Art and Industry by Herbert Read
Faber & Faber, London

Prehistoric Art by J. Poulik
Spring Books, London

Primitive Art by E. O. Christensen
The Viking Press, Inc., New York
Thames & Hudson, London

The Thinking Eye by Paul Klee

Naturen Som Formgivare by Bertel Bager
En botanisk kinststudie
Nordisk Rotogravyr, Stockholm

The Dawn of Civilisation, ed. Stuart Piggott
Thames & Hudson, London

Volkskunst in Europa by H. T. H. Bossert
Verlag Ernst Wasmuth, A.G., Berlin

Shaker Furniture by Edward and Faith Andrews
Dover Publications, New York

Art in European Architecture by Paul Damaz
Reinhold Publishing Corporation, New York

Cahiers d'Art, 1948. I. 'Ceramiques de Picasso'
14 Rue du Dragon, Paris

Two Thousand Years of Oriental Ceramics by
Fujio Koyama and John Figgess
Thames & Hudson, London

New Bauhaus Books by Moholy Nagy

Ceramica del Levante Español Siglos Medievales
by M Gonzalez Marti. Loza
Editorial Labor. Spain 1944.

The Faber Monograph Series
Each book covers a definite period of Ceramic
History
Faber & Faber, London

A Picture History of English Pottery by
Griselda Lewis
Vista Books, London

Arts de L'Amerique by Raoul d'Harcourt
Arts du Monde, Les Editions du Chene, Paris

Pottery of Tomimoto by Tadasi Naito

Never Leave Well Alone by Raymond Loewy

Technics and Civilisation by Lewis Mumford

European Ceramic Art by W. B. Honey
Faber & Faber, London

Prehistoric Pottery in China by G. D. Wu
Kegan Paul, London

*The Ceramic Art of China and other Countries of
the Far East* by W. B. Honey
Faber & Faber, London

Guide to the Collection of Tiles
Victoria & Albert Museum, London

A Potter's Book by Bernard Leach
Faber & Faber, London

Chemistry and Technical Books

Inorganic Chemistry by E. J. Holmyard
Edward Arnold, Publishers, London

Modern Inorganic Chemistry by J. W. Mellor
Longmans, London

Ceramic Colours and Pottery Decoration by
Kenneth Shaw
Maclaren, London

Clay and Glazes for the Potter by D. Rhodes
Pitman, London

Ceramic Glazes by C. W. Parmelee
Industrial Publications Inc., Chicago 3

The Technique of Pottery by Dora Billington
Batsford, London

The Manual of Practical Potting by C. F. Binns
Scott Greenwood (1907)

Modern Pottery Manufacture by H. N. Bose
Ceramic Publishing House
Bhagalpur, India

North Staffordshire Technical College
Library Catalogue. Technical Press

Business Methods
Rural Industries Bureau, London

Professional Practice for Designers by
Dorothy Goslett
Batsford, London

Formulario y Practicas de Ceramica by J. L. Artigas
Grastavo Gili, Spain

The Pottery Gazette Reference Book is extremely useful for lists of suppliers, etc.

Introduction

People beginning ceramics in the post-war era have inherited the sound tradition established earlier by Bernard Leach and his followers; and Bernard Leach, in his turn, was inspired by the works of Morris and Lethaby, to whom 'truth to materials' with all its implications was of prime importance.

Today, there are a number of ceramists, Lucy Rie amongst them, who are continuing to enrich this tradition by producing individual pieces of domestic ware in a highly personal style. But, with all the great changes – social, economic and artistic – that have taken place since World War II, how many ceramists have sought to extend tradition to meet the new needs and conditions of the present day?

When the restrictions of war and rationing were over, the great cry and demand was for colour, to be used with daring and verve in ceramics, fabrics, interiors and a host of allied fields and activities. With this desire for colour there developed a greater appreciation of natural surfaces and materials, from wood to stone, where textures blended and contrasted. No longer were purely individual pots, and, to a limited extent, hand-made domestic ware the only accepted products of the potter. There were new uses and far greater opportunities for ceramic work than before.

During this period of change Picasso with his daring, invention, colour-sense and imagination, shattered and shocked the traditionalist potters with his experiments in ceramics. While his approach was obviously more that of the painter, he added fresh life and a new direction to ceramics, and from his activities stemmed many schools of thought and expression which flowered in the 'fifties. Ceramists found that their values needed drastic revision, while at the same time they endeavoured to retain an openness of mind and an integrity in the use of their materials.

Was British industry alive to what was happening, and did it revitalize its tradition with fresh ideas and imaginative thought? Alas, with few exceptions, it does not appear so, nor were most of the individual potters prepared to co-operate, when industry ignored – and still ignores – them and the contribution they could make. As a result, the world now wants only our traditional wares, and shops elsewhere for good modern design.

Now let us look at what has happened beyond these shores. In Scandinavia, management has used ideas intelligently, and employed the best potters, consequently gaining them a world-wide reputation. In Japan the work of the potter is prized above that of the painter,

7

and the proceeds from the sale of one pot can supply all the needs of a distinguished potter for at least three months. In America there is a demand for imaginative and lively ceramics; and in Australia, we are told, the demand for individual pottery far exceeds the supply.

Here in England many small industrial firms have closed or been forced to merge with others, in order to survive economically. And science, in the name of uniformity for mass production, has eliminated much of the natural richness and variety in many raw materials. These added factors, combined with competition from plastics, make it essential that ceramists should have a high standard of design – but this has yet to be achieved.

Too few of us are alive to the implications of living fully in the present. Yet, today the ceramist may be commissioned to supply, say, large pottery containers, individual pieces for a board room, perhaps an external ceramic feature for a wall, even asked to advise on suitable ware for the restaurant or canteen; and all for one client and one building. Here, surely, is a cue for the future; there is a growing demand for the variety and richness of ceramics that few other materials can replace.

This is a situation that can be exploited, but only after careful thought and planning, coupled with the acquisition of ceramic experience and the widest possible knowledge. And, to succeed, we must look further back into history to find a wider application of ceramics for stimulating us today. But though, for a time, some of us may strive to fulfil these needs, the day must surely come, as it has in other countries, when industry, with its wealth and resources, will combine with the ceramist, recognise the real contribution that each can make, and work out a plan for co-operation.

The illustrations in this book have been chosen in an effort to show just how varied the techniques and uses of ceramics can be and, too, the part played by colour and contrast.

1 · Clays

Before hoping to tackle all the exciting prospects offered in the field of pottery today, the beginner must have a natural sympathy and feeling for his materials, and to this must be added a lively imagination. He must aim to be an artist and a craftsman, with a skilled control of all pottery techniques, a knowledge of chemistry and, last but not least (if his aim is professional as against amateur), he must be able to develop a practical business sense.

In this book, I shall endeavour to cover all these aspects – many of them in detail. But before embarking, it is essential to say something about the background and properties of clay itself – the ceramist's basic material.

Composition

We are told by the geologists that 90% of the bulk of the earth's surface is composed of five minerals: Alumina, Silica, Lime, Carbon and Iron. Further, they state that the average composition of rocks constituting the earth's crust to a depth of ten miles is as follows:

Silica	59·14%
Alumina	15·34%
Ferric & Ferrous Oxide	6·88%
Calcium Oxide	5·08%
Sodium Oxide	3·84%
Magnesium Oxide	3·49%
Potassium Oxide	3·13%
Water	1·15%
Titanium Oxide	1·05%
	99·10
All others	·90
	100·00

It will be seen that almost 75% of the above is made up of silica and alumina, and it is therefore, not surprising to discover that these two minerals constitute, on average, some 80% of the bulk of most clays. Clays are divided into two categories, primary and secondary.

Primary clays

Primary clays are those remaining in their forming grounds, which are not numerous throughout the world. The present, most strongly-held theory is that the primary, or china, clay was formed in the later stages of the earth's cooling some 300,000,000 years ago, by hydrothermal action upon areas of granitic rocks. China clay consists of kaolinite, a hydrated silicate of aluminium which, as described above, is the product of decomposed felspar, one of the chief constituents of granitic igneous rocks. It is interesting to learn that, while to potters English china clay is not very plastic, Chinese Kaolin did possess a greater plasticity. This is a reason why the Chinese achieved such outstanding results in their making of fine porcelain.

Secondary plastic clays

Secondary clays of the ball and stoneware varieties are also derived from decomposed felspathic rocks, which through the action of rivers and natural erosion were deposited away from their forming grounds. Hence the term 'secondary'. Many ball clays are black in colour and more plastic because of their organic content which, with their particular laminatory structure, makes them highly plastic when water is added. Ball clay is of comparatively recent origin, being some 35,000,000 years old.

The other, more red-firing secondary clay deposits widespread throughout the world, were formed much earlier and possibly about the same time as china clay deposits. Secondary clays vary in colour from white to cream, and from pale pink to red, and black. The black is due to vegetable matter, which burns out during firing, leaving the clay white, red or buff. The more common red clays are more or less rock-like in appearance when dug, becoming soft and plastic when wet, but remaining brittle and hard when dry.

Because of the wide varieties and properties of clays available from natural deposits, it is seldom that the nearest deposit will suit your particular needs. As many secondary clays contain certain impurities, such as quartz rock, mica, limestone particles, and other minerals, it is easier for many of us working today to use prepared bodies, or natural clays of reasonably consistent composition that have needed only to be cleaned. Many potters do use these cleaned clays from a number of suppliers, as well as standard prepared bodies.

Prepared bodies

The basis of these, if buff or white, is a very plastic ball clay, to which has been added china clay, china stone, and flint, in varying proportions. A suitable recipe would be as follows:

EARTHENWARE CLAY

Ball clay	30%
China clay	20%
Cornish stone	15%
Flint	35%

Red clays according to their prospective uses may be prepared in various ways. Some are merely dug and cleaned, while others may have additions of flint, or sand and grog (ground biscuit ware), or even a proportion of prepared white or buff clay.

The fusing and vitrifying of clay in the kiln is caused by alkaline fluxes (page 69) present in the body, and is also greatly affected by the size of the clay particles. In ball clay these agents are mainly sodium and potassium compounds. In red clays, these alkalis are present together with magnesium and calcium, in addition to iron oxide – a strong flux common to all red bodies. This means that most red clays as a general rule vitrify (page 69) around 1060°C, though some may fire as low as 1000°C.

PREPARED STONEWARE AND PORCELAIN BODIES In stoneware bodies the proportion of fluxes is necessarily smaller, being balanced by the addition of more refractory ingredients, such as sand, flint, grog, or china clay. The fluxes come from the ball clay and the china stone. Although china clay is a primary clay, it contains no fluxes, owing to thorough washing at the clay pits.

STONEWARE BODIES TO FIRE AT 1250–1300°C

Ball clay	25%	35%	35%
China clay	25%	20%	20%
China stone	25%	25%	—
Sand (silver)	25%	20%	25%
Felspar	—	—	20%

When preparing the above, add the sand after other ingredients have been sieved.

PORCELAIN RECIPES

China clay	55%	China clay	50%
Bentonite	5%	Ball clay	17%
Felspar	25%	China stone	25%
Quartz (not flint)	15%	Flint	8%

Cost

The price of clays can range widely from the cost of cleaned natural clays, to that of specially prepared bodies. Remember that the cost of freight can be calculated as being an additional 50% of the price. For an important project it may be necessary to use an expensive clay, but the cost will still form only a very minor percentage of the estimated cost of the project. The most expensive form of clay is a china casting slip, because of the high cost of the bone ash – the main chemical constituent of which is calcium phosphate which is prepared from calcined animal bones.

Storing clay

If you have a damp cellar, or basement, there will be no storage problem, and your clay can easily be kept damp for months. When this is not the case, keep it wrapped in sheets of polythene, and store in a zinc-lined, airtight container, or large metal or plastic dustbin.

You will find that even these precautions may not prevent drying, so keep a damp sack or cloth permanently covering the clay. Do not use containers that will rust, even if the clay is wrapped in polythene.

Preparing clay

Whatever your technique of wedging clay may be, the need for thorough preparation cannot be stressed too emphatically. Wedging is the technique of mixing or kneading moist clay by hand so as to give it the same consistency throughout. This form of preparation is always

1 Cutting of clay into slices during wedging, to check its condition; then placing each piece on edge and flattening with the palm of the hand before re-wedging.

essential. Take care not to place your prepared clay on dry plaster, wood or other porous surfaces, or in a draught. The clay can quickly become unevenly dry, thus impairing your work.

When wedging your clay, cut well and often with a wire, as it is surprising what foreign bodies find their way into clay – from razor blades and sponges, to engagement rings and match sticks! If clay has been prepared and left for some time, it should always be re-wedged before it is used. To check whether clay has been sufficiently wedged, cut it in half with a strong wire, or nylon thread, and you will see how even in texture the clay has become. You may also check its readiness for use by drawing your finger across its surface, whereupon any variation in the clay may be felt.

Should clay become dirty with particles of plaster or other foreign matter, the quickest way to clean it is to force it away from you along the wedging bench from a pile in front of you, with the palm of the hand. Where it becomes thin on the bench, any foreign particles become visible, and are easily removed. If the clay is soft, it is surprising how quickly a large quantity of it can be cleaned by this method.

Unevenly prepared clay can crack or shatter during firing, due to stresses set up between the stratified hard and soft layers, as plastic clays have a laminatory structure. I have yet to see a pot that shattered or cracked as a result of air bubbles in the clay. However, if clay ware is fired too quickly, or the ware is insufficiently dry on being packed into the kiln, moisture in the clay will quickly change to steam. This does not have time to escape in the normal way, but expands rapidly and can cause complete shattering, or blow large flat pieces from the sides of the ware.

DAMPING Clay that has become too dry or pots that have dried out should be broken into reasonably small pieces, placed in a large shallow container and just covered with water. Leave for a day or so till the water has had time to penetrate and soften the clay without making it excessively soft. Mix by wedging on a plaster slab or on a wooden bench, but if the clay is still too soft, leave it in a pile to be air-dried before wedging again.

2 Mixing and cleaning of soft clay by forcing it away with the palm of the hand; where it becomes thin on the bench any foreign matter can be seen and removed.

TIRED CLAY Clay that has been in constant use for throwing practice may suddenly collapse, splitting as it folds. This is called 'tired' clay, from having been overworked. It should be stored for some time to regain its former condition, or be mixed with fresh clay.

DRYING CLAY Excessively moist clay is best dried on slabs of plaster, or in large shallow plaster dish moulds, which are also suitable for drying out slip (a fluid mixture of clay and water, described in Chapter 5). Keep the slabs of plaster, or moulds, on bricks to allow the moisture absorbed from the clay to evaporate, thus preventing the floor or bench from rotting. Drying techniques depend very much on climate, the quantity of clay immediately available, and the amount of clay being used. This will obviously be a minor problem in a production pottery – unless you prepare your own clay-bodies, and then adequate facilities will have been provided. The drying of clay wares to be ready for firing is described in Chapter 8.

Shrinkage and recording details of clay in use

When setting up professionally, it is advisable to use only a limited number of clay bodies, for both practical and economic reasons. These clays should be thoroughly tested for percentage of shrinkage, vitrifying temperature, and temperatures in excess of those advocated, in case at any time the ware should be overfired.

To test the shrinkage of a clay, roll out a long coil the thickness of your thumb and cut off a 10-in length. In this way any shrinkage can be calculated as a percentage, should you need it for calculations. For some projects it is essential to calculate a series of shrinkages, when the ceramic has to fit a given space. Once the percentage of shrinkage is known, the following formula is very helpful.

To calculate what initial length a piece of clay must be to shrink to a given length when the percentage shrinkage of the clay is known:

$$\text{let } a = \text{initial length of clay in inches}$$
$$\text{let } b = \text{final length of clay in inches}$$
$$\text{let } x\% = \text{percentage shrinkage}$$

Then by definition shrinkage $= \left(a \times \dfrac{x}{100} \right)$ inches

Because initial length of clay $-$ shrinkage $=$ final length of clay, we have

$$a - \left(a \times \frac{x}{100} \right) = b$$

transposing we get $\quad a \left(1 - \dfrac{x}{100} \right) = b = a \left(\dfrac{100 - x}{100} \right)$

$$\text{and} \quad a = b \left(\frac{100}{100 - x} \right)$$

e.g. If shrinkage is 7·3%
and final length is 40·625 ins, or 3 ft $4\frac{5}{8}$ ins

$$\text{then } a = 40 \cdot 625 \left(\frac{100}{100 - 7 \cdot 3} \right)$$

$$\therefore \quad \text{Initial length} \quad a = 40 \cdot 625 \times \frac{100}{92 \cdot 7}$$

$$= 43 \cdot 82 \text{ ins}$$

$$= 43\tfrac{13}{16}$$

$$= 3 \text{ ft } 7\tfrac{13}{16} \text{ ins}$$

Record the different shrinkage between moist, and dry unfired clay, together with that recorded in the biscuit firing. This is found to be approximately two to one, with the greater shrinkage before firing, when some 20% of water by weight has been dried from the moist clay. The percentage of shrinkage from moist to biscuit-fired clay should then be calculated and recorded for future reference.

2 · Beginning with clay

As people, we westerners have largely neglected our inherent tactile sense, and the development of these senses is, naturally, of prime importance to the ceramist. A plastic malleable quality distinguishes his material and the results, from those of any other art or craft form. It is interesting to note that when a small child is first given a piece of soft clay, he will pinch off small pieces and press them on to a surface in the manner of a Seurat painting, thus instinctively exploring and defining the nature of the material. Until this quality is inherent in the work of the ceramist the results will lack true conviction; and it is wiser to begin by fully exploring what can be achieved with just clay and the hands before becoming seduced by the fascinating technique of throwing on a wheel. Throwing is best learnt from highly skilled craftsmen; for good throwing is a difficult technique, though it appears easy to the untutored eye. Students should first explore and experiment as widely as possible with the medium before narrowing their field of activity.

Before discussing experimental exercises we should consider the different types of clay with their various uses.

Ceramic articles can be made in many ways. They may be cast in a plaster mould, made mechanically with jigger and jolly, hand-thrown, stamped, or dust-pressed in a metal or plastic mould, coiled or slabbed, press moulded or shaped, or extruded. For some methods a plastic clay is necessary for its physical properties; for others a semi- or non-plastic clay is equally possible. Plasticity is defined as the ability of a substance, when damp, to retain indefinitely the particular shape into which it has been squeezed, pressed, forced or rolled. Ball clay or bentonite may be added to increase the plasticity of a clay.

Perhaps the best method of comparing the plasticity of clays is to roll them into long thin coils, when the less plastic will break and crumble while still thick. All clays must be moist for use, except when dust-pressing, and even then a percentage of water content is necessary to aid adhesion. A fair degree of plasticity is essential for the techniques of rolling, slabbing and pressing, and the more plastic clays are also needed for throwing or the technique becomes impossible. Coarse materials, however, may be added to an extremely plastic clay and still make throwing possible. For both industrial and individual hand-building of large forms, an open coarse-textured clay is preferred, with just sufficient binding for easy handling, though for many other industrial processes a fine-textured clay is required. In the making of jigger and jolly articles, ball clay is needed to give mechanical

strength for handling, in both wet and dry states. But, while in earthenware casting slips ball clay does give strength for handling, it is more useful for making casting slips chemically stable.

As a general rule, delicate forms need a fine-textured clay, and thick robust forms a coarse clay. The type of clay used will therefore depend on the following factors:

a Temperature at which it must be fired
b Method of manufacture
c Degree of handling when making
d Resistance to sudden changes of heat
e Required mechanical strength when fired
f Possible availability of raw materials combined with cost

Some ball clays are much more plastic than others; so only a little may be necessary to give the required plasticity to certain prepared bodies.

For those who wish to cover a wide field of ceramic techniques, it is essential to have experience and an understanding of the many different clays and their uses. They may often have to make decisions regarding the most suitable form of ceramic for a particular purpose: for example, what clay should be used for ceramic panels to be fitted in metal door-pushes for an office block, or for large plant containers for external use. As a general rule the conception of the shape will dictate the method to be used in its making.

First exercises
Roll into balls with the hands various sized pieces of clay. Roll them spherical, roll them assymetrical. Roll them and press them firmly between the palms, and squeeze them between the thumb and forefinger.

Place a medium-sized ball in the palm of one hand and slowly and gently press the free thumb into the ball of clay. Try this with balls of varying size. Take a ball and, slowly and rhythmically, with a revolving movement, squeeze between the first fingers and thumbs of both hands till it becomes a flat, circular, even disc or pancake. This teaches control and the feeling of thickness, which is the basis of all hrowing, hand shaping and building. Practise this with different sizes and types of clay, and you will soon discover the variation in plasticity of coarse and fine clays. When control is acquired repeat the exercise, but this time taper the clay towards the edges till you have a hape like a shallow discus or top.

While one of the circular flat slabs is still moist, roll it up like

3 Series of exercises using only the hands and fingers to roll, pinch, squeeze and shape the clay.

1 'Footballers and Fishes', clay panel by Simon Clark, aged 3.

2 'The Cocktail Party' by Sophia Gray. This shows a child's ability to use imaginatively a selection of pottery modelling-tools together with contrasting coloured clays.

3 Finished area of pattern from last stage of Plate 4.

4 Design progression, starting with a small plain cylinder of plaster to which incisions were added until the desired unity of design was achieved. An excellent method for exploring and developing a sense of design and decoration for those who find it particularly difficult.

5 Three pinched pots by Nancy Denine, a student.

6 Stoneware panel, showing an interesting use of folded clay, by Julia Brown.

7 Sea-worn stones showing their dominant structure.

9 Drawing from an insect and an arrangement of shapes from it, by Eileen Nesbit.

10 Ancient Peruvian jar, shaped and painted with a vigorous simplicity and directness. *British Museum.*

11 Coiled jar from Arizona, A.D. 1200, where the pattern is a direct result of the way in which the pot was made. *British Museum.*

12 Ancient Peruvian jar of superb form and decoration. *British Museum.*

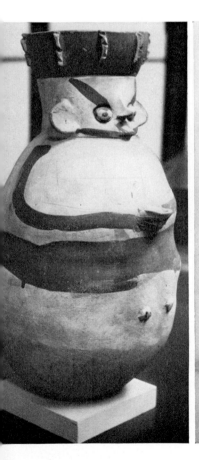  

13 Spouted bowl from the Ubaid Period, 4000–3500 B.C., with vigorously painted geometric pattern. *British Museum.*

14 Black-and-white ware jar from Arizona, probably Pueblo III period, with painted geometric pattern. *British Museum.*

15 Stoneware bowl by Lucie Rie, showing a deliberate use of metallic particles in the body to add richness to the glaze.

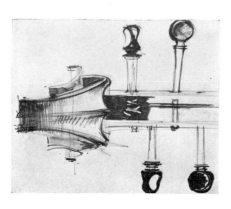 

16 Pencil drawing of a violin handle by Eileen Nesbit.

17 Design based on the drawing.

18 Porcelain beaker decorated with a design derived from the above.

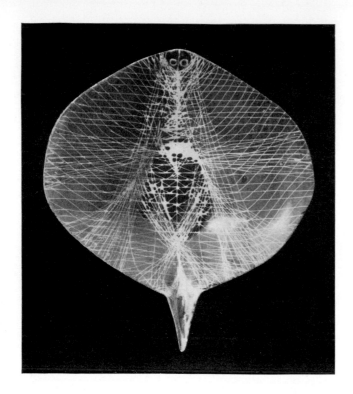

19 Fine fish-shaped dish by James Tower showing his mastery in the use of line.

20 Jar with majolica brush decoration by Alan Caiger-Smith.

21 Drawing of fish section by Patricia O'Hare, a student.

22 Sculptural Terra-cotta by James Tower. By courtesy Gimpel Fils Gallery.

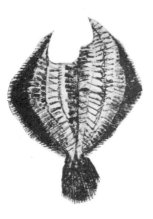

23 Large jar decorated by Picasso; shown at the exhibition 'Prehistory to Picasso' at the Goldsmiths' College, lent by Mr A. Zwemmer, from his collection.

24 Slip-cast llama brushed with black pigment and then biscuit fired. The decoration is produced by sgraffito through a white glaze, before refiring; by Ann Wynn Reeves.

25 Slip-cast hen and chicken. Here the unfired clay is rubbed with wax and pigment brushed on. After biscuit firing they are glazed with a majolica glaze; by Ann Wynn Reeves.

26 Two incised jigger-and-jolly moulds.

27 Dish from mould in Plate 26 with design now in relief. This will be pigmented in the raw clay state, hand coloured and glazed when biscuited.

28 Slip-cast money pigs individually decorated with coloured glaze and pigment on a white glaze. Shape designed by Paul Gell and decorated by Ann Wynn Reeves.

4 Flat strips of clay, coiled to form a composite pattern.

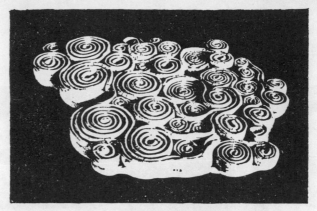

a carpet to test its strength and flexibility. Continue by rolling clay between the hands and on a flat surface, into as many shapes as you can, ranging from the sphere to the cylinder.

Work in both red and white clay till a number of shapes have accumulated. Select some of these and place them on one of the thin circular discs of clay as a three dimensional composition, all the while relating and contrasting one with another, till the whole becomes a unified design. In this case, each unit may be considered as a three-dimensional element, which might later be taken as a maquette for a large hand-built free standing shape.

In the same context rolled shapes may be built on the disc of clay like a totem pole, giving a contrast to the shorter varying shapes.

Clay shapes range from flat and round, to long and thin; so rolling a piece into a long coil is just another method of squeezing clay. This is not an easy technique, and should be performed gently with the fingers. They should always move outwards from the centre when rolling, so that the thickness is always rolled out from the centre of the coil.

From a given piece of clay, now roll a coil as thin and as long as your skill allows. Next

5 Exercise using rolled shapes for a composition arranged on a flat disc of clay.

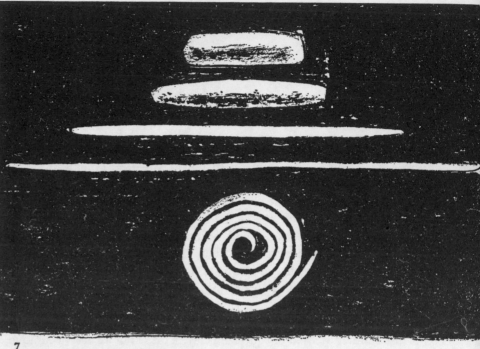

6 Vertical structure made from hand-rolled shapes.
7 Progressive stages in rolling a coil of clay.

take medium coils, break them into varying lengths and join each to form a circle. These may be gently squeezed to make open cylinders, or alternatively, lengths of coil can be squeezed flat and then joined. Flattened coils can also be rolled into a spiral (see fig. 4).

The study of proportion, interval, outline and relative volume are essential if ceramics are to make a contribution within an architectural context. Certain simple rolled shapes, as well as solid cylinders, may be dipped in black or white slip according to the colour of the clay. This should divide the forms horizontally at varying intervals of intended proportions. Even open cylinders can be dipped and built into a column to develop this sense. A further exercise would be dipping in contrasting slip, at angles other than vertical or horizontal lines to the form. In this way the cross section of a form becomes far more apparent.

It becomes obvious that even at this stage we must begin to consider pattern and texture. We find that a sense of form, an awareness of pattern and decoration, a tactile sympathy with the material, and the urge to build must all be related and developed at the same time. While it is agreed that it is undesirable to decorate all shapes, this should be a matter of choice and not of inability, as is so often the case.

18

8 Cylinders of contrasting width and height, arranged on a flat disc of clay; an exercise in three-dimensional composition.

9 Similar exercise to fig. 8 viewed from above.

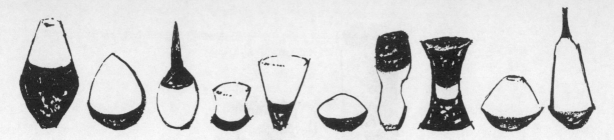

10 (a) Range of small, rolled, white clay forms, dipped in black slip.

Unless there is a parallel growth and development of these qualities a form of ceramic schizophrenia can occur. Form and texture could therefore be combined as follows:

Make a series of solid clay cylinders and gently roll one, when not too soft, across a textured surface such as coarsely woven linen or a cocoanut fibre doormat. Repeat this on a variety of surfaces and study the relation of the pattern to the form. In the same way a flat strip of clay can be pressed on a textured surface and then joined, as suggested earlier, to make an open cylinder of patterned clay. And taller, plain, solid cylinders can be placed

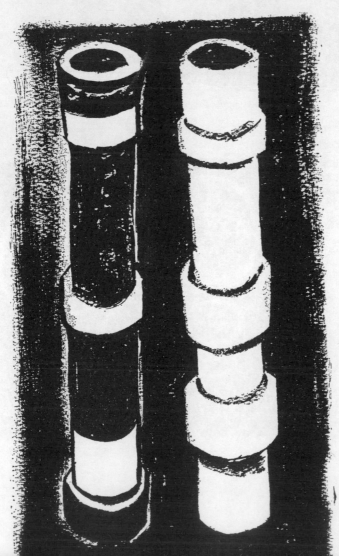

11 Cylinders of varying height, colour and dimension, joined and built as vertical forms.

12 *Right* Cylinders of solid clay rolled across textured surfaces. ▶

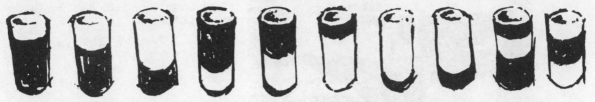

10 (b) Range of uniform, small, white clay cylinders, dipped in black slip; an exercise in progressive proportion.

near or inside a series of these to form, once again, a composition of related shapes with different surfaces.

Textures in clay

With a wooden rolling pin roll out flat, smooth areas of clay approximately $12 \times 12 \times \frac{1}{2}$ in thick. Take any tools you may be using plus a piece of old comb, kitchen utensils and anything that makes, when pressed into the clay, what you consider to be an interesting mark or texture. Do not forget that the use of your fingers alone can give a wide range of patterns to a clay surface. The best of these you may use later as a basis for ideas when decorating three dimensional shapes.

While working on a flat surface take a stick of white chalk or a cylinder of plaster and incise or cut a line into its length. Roll it across the surface of the clay and observe the result. Now cut added marks to this line and roll again. This should be continued and the design progress till you are satisfied that the balance of the composition has been achieved (pl. 4). Motifs can be cut into the ends of the chalk or plaster and then pressed into the clay. This technique has been used since prehistoric times, and even today has been developed in such a way by industrial potteries in Scandinavia as to enhance the surface of their wares. Many studio potters working today use this and similar techniques to decorate both stoneware and earthenware.

While working on the foregoing exercises, the student should have a sense of complete personal involvement. It is therefore extremely important to have the help of a good teacher, with whom he can discuss the work and who will suggest ways in which certain ideas can be further developed or even combined. This also applies when developing ideas for decoration, as these suggestions are only a beginning, to act as a stimulus for further personal discoveries and development.

13 Large hand-built dish, by Gillian Lowndes.

3 · From exercises to forms

Once confidence in handling clay on a small scale has been achieved, the building of larger, simple forms should follow. This may be approached in two ways: firstly by making a series of solid, rolled, squeezed or shaped forms and selecting one to be greatly enlarged by hand building or coiling (described on page 38); secondly by drawing a series of shapes, freely and to intended size, on large sheets of paper in brush charcoal or a similar medium. Obviously a combination of the two methods is the most satisfactory.

The advantage of beginning in this way is that the student has some idea of what the end result should be. He will often find that modifications will suggest themselves or be necessary as the form grows. While building a large clay form, it will be necessary for the clay to harden slightly in order to support the weight; but it should not become too dry. While it is drying, the top edge should be kept moist with a damp cloth or plastic sheet, before continuing to finish the shape. With this method there is time to think and consider while the shape is being made whereas, with throwing, sureness and speed is all important. From this it can be seen that form in ceramics has much in common with sculpture, and there are many people today who practise sculpture and ceramics, often combining ideas from both.

While waiting for a large form to harden, another method to practise is hand-shaping or making a pinched pot. Do not attempt too large a piece at first, but as skill improves increase the size of the ball of clay. These pots are made by squeezing rhythmically and gently with a revolving motion between the thumb and fingers of either hand. For larger shapes the palm of one hand and the fingers of the other can be used in squeezing the walls of the clay. For beginners, the most common fault is the edge cracking, and this can be largely overcome by making the edge fairly thin in the early stages. Do not wet the surface with water if it becomes a little dry, but prevent this by starting with moister clay.

When these pinched-pots have become drier they can, if wished, be decorated by some of the techniques explored earlier, or left undecorated. Again the shape of the intended finished form should determine the method of handling from the very beginning, and the angle at which the fingers and thumb are working: vertical for a deep shape and more

14 Tall hand-built forms, by Gillian Lowndes.

15 Four stages in the making of a pinched
bowl.

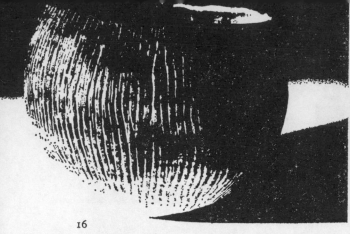

16 Pinched pot by Ann Wynn Reeves, with linear incised decoration.
17 Another pinched pot by Ann Wynn Reeves, with an asymmetrical, incised, abstract pattern.

horizontal for shallower forms (fig. 18). Thus one is putting into practice some of the ideas explored in the earlier exercise.

When making large shapes, other methods can be to select a simple natural form of any size and directly build or develop a large clay shape from it, or to start by making large drawings based on the form. The more symmetrical or circular the section of the form as a whole, the greater affinity it will have with throwing. With hand building, therefore, the opportunity should be taken to explore the relationships of asymmetric form.

18 Drawings showing the relationship between the initial cross-section and the finished form of a deep and a shallow pinched pot.

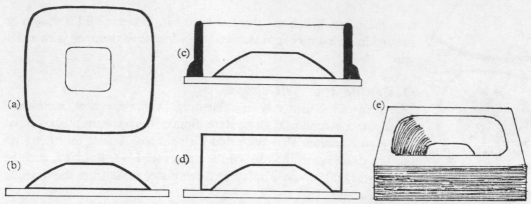

(a)

(c)

(e)

(b)

(d)

19 (a & b) Plan and elevation of a modelled, solid clay shape, from which a dish mould is to be cast. (c) Supporting clay wall, ready for pouring in plaster. (d) Cross-section of cast plaster-mould. (e) Mould ready for use.

Pressed shapes

While there are exceptions, there is a general rule that one does not attempt to make shapes by hand building, that can more easily be made on a potters' wheel. As a consequence, most dishes made from rolled clay pressed into a mould tend to be anything but circular in plan. The simplest and most direct method of making a dish mould is to model with soft clay the required shape in relief, cast it in plaster and then roll and press clay into the mould when dry. The clay for making the model should be well wedged and smoothed with a flexible metal strip in the final stages of shaping.

Rolling clay

Clay for dishes can be cut in layers from a large block, or each piece can be rolled from a lump of prepared clay. It is best rolled on a heavy, stiff piece of sacking or cloth, and lifted and separated from the cloth regularly while rolling. First flatten the clay with the hand and then roll, beginning always from the centre and working outward in one direction and

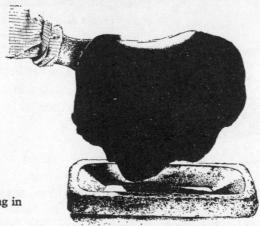

20 Rolled clay held across the arm ready for laying in the plaster mould.

then the other. When the clay has been laid in the mould it should be pressed in with a rubber kidney and the edges then trimmed with a thin wire.

Designing the dish shape
The form of the dish may be influenced by the exercises, mentioned already, where solid oval forms were dipped into a contrasting coloured slip, giving sections that suggested dish shapes. These, together with full size drawings of the plan of the dish, could be combined, and the clay mould built up on a heavy card template, made from the drawing of the plan (fig. 19).

Combining forms
Here again one sees the importance of developing an idea on a small scale. Two shallow pinched shapes of equal diameter may be joined at the edge to give a hollow, shallow, form, which should be pierced before firing, to allow the air to escape. This can be repeated using a deep pot and a shallow dish, both having the same diameter where joined. Both hollow shapes may now be joined with slip after partial hardening and, naturally, after careful consideration. It is now easy to repeat the exercise with dishes made from one or two press moulds, and to develop the idea in a variety of ways. Following this, two or more open or enclosed forms should be joined with slip or clay, or, for instance, a slabbed rectangular shape or shapes be joined to ones made from the dish mould. If the plaster mould is too restricting, the clay may be shaped in a bowl of damp sand which has been scooped out to give the required shape, and the clay either laid or worked in.

In all these exercises the ceramist is acquiring and expanding his vocabulary. Therefore, in the same way that piano exercises are not played in the concert hall, the student of ceramics will and should make many forms and articles that may have no immediate function or sale. This experience, however, will be invaluable for his development, or for future work as a professional. Here, as in most activities, one learns the vocabulary either before or at the same time that one begins to use it to express ideas, and until you can control the medium the results will lack coherence.

Form
Form can be defined as the solid reality of objects surrounding, or, surrounded by space.

In assessing form, the impulse is often to feel it. How often do you hear a young child being told, 'Leave it alone, don't touch', when all he is doing is discovering, through his tactile sense? When studying form,

21 Side elevation and plan of three different forms partially dipped in a slip of contrasting colour to give ideas for shapes of dish moulds. These can be developed using both plan and elevation.

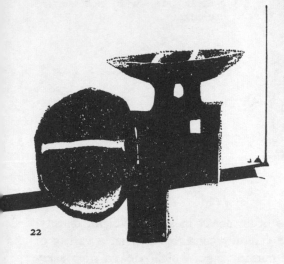

22

22 Exercise in construction; joining curved and rectangular forms. Work from an L.C.C. teachers' course.

23 Joining shallow and deep hand-shaped dishes, of the same diameter.

24 Exercise in joining three, hollow, hand-built forms by David Ward, first year student.

23

24

one must be constantly aware of the wholeness of an object in space. Weight, density, changing structure and cross-section should be carefully considered. What a variety of form, balance, section and line, we have in the human figure, which, viewed from every possible angle shows a thousand profiles. Of how many things do we tend to see only one aspect, or at the most two? In the study of form the student should draw with this in mind, otherwise the result will be little more than a recorded outline. Draw tree trunks, every aspect of such things as a walnut shell, solid forms of fruit and seeds, together with their cross-sections and inner structures. Observe rock structures and stones, the flight of birds and the movement of water. Study symmetric balance and asymmetric balance. And when observing and drawing natural forms, try to discover and understand what are the underlying natural laws of growth and interaction which determine the final result as we see it. While natural phenomena are a source of stimulus to the imagination, the object as a whole can never be recreated. However, one or several aspects may be taken from their context and developed to create a new form or pattern. It has been said that Nature and Art are two different things and that through art we express our conception of what nature is not. Paul Klee expressed this another way. 'The artist', he said, 'does not think the appearances of nature so all-important as the realists do. He does not feel tied to realities, because it is not the outcome of the creative forces of nature which interests him so much as the form-giving forces themselves.'

Now let us briefly consider past and present forms. We find that they range from heavy modelled Islamic tiles, to shallow richly decorated and coloured Persian dishes, tall elegant Sung vases, earthy prehistoric urns, as well as superbly modelled T'ang horses. Here we see a rich variety of surface treatments and glaze effects; plain cylinders with excellent proportions, which by another hand might be dull and lifeless. Observe the vitality and bursting quality of a vigorously thrown shape or, alternatively, one that has dignity and serenity. Observe, too, those forms enhanced by a gay luxuriance of earthenware colours, so difficult to control yet capable of endless variety, and compare them with stoneware forms with their rich quietly mysterious quality of glaze, and bodies of textured hardness like the sea-worn stones on an ocean beach – one formed by the hand of man and heated with a controlling hand, the other a product of fierce natural causes when the world was formed. Notice the refined elegance of porcelain and china that have the delicacy of

28

26 Twig and leaves illustrating the sharply contrasting qualities of line and shape.

27 Drawing showing the internal linear structure of the leaves shown in fig. 28.

28 Solid outlined leaf shapes of fig. 27 where a fluid varying outline contrasts with the more rigid internal structure.

26

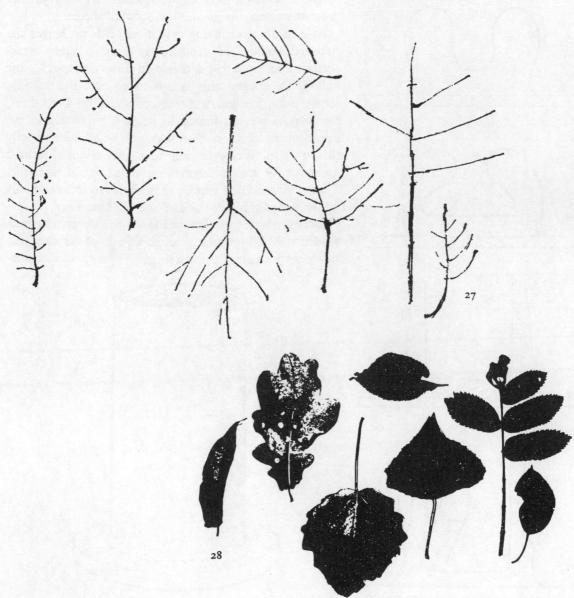

27

28

29

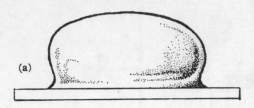

(a)

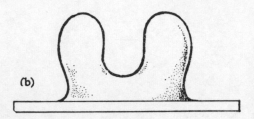

(b)

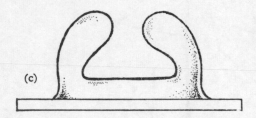

(c)

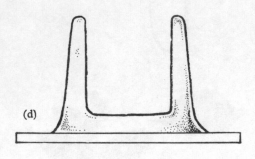

(d)

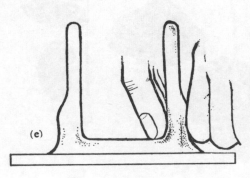

(e)

sea-shells and of the shells of rare and exotic birds' eggs, combined with a hardness of steel. All this must be absorbed, felt and understood.

Throwing and its development

Throwing is, basically, the technique of shaping, with the hands, a ball of soft clay on a rotating wheel. The hands control and shape the clay, which is being thrown outwards by the centrifugal force of the spinning wheelhead. The faster the wheel, the greater the outward thrust.

As a result of changing conditions, it is no longer the standard method of production, even in many small potteries. In those that still rely on thrown shapes for the bulk of their wares the pace is tough, and the quantity required for economic survival is formidable. For others, throwing is more a means to an end, or an aid in the development of ideas that may not result in a strictly thrown form. Whatever your aims, it is essential to have a respect for and understanding of the art of throwing. I am convinced that certain sensibilities to form can only be developed through the medium of throwing.

Once the basic technique of throwing has been mastered, students should progress through a series of exercises that cover every aspect of thrown forms. These should include

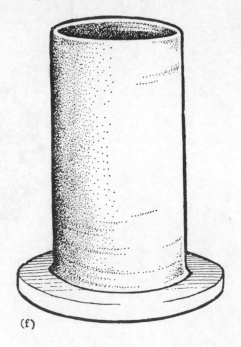

(f)

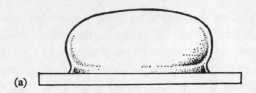
(a)

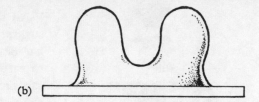
(b)

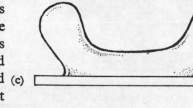
(c)

cylinders of every width, height, thickness and size; cylinders with as varied a selection of top edges as possible, that will add a richness and variety to the form; spheres and ovoids, with all the variations possible; followed by spheres with thick necks and tall necks; shallow dishes and bowls, deep bowls and open beakers; cylinders and spheres with lids that have sunken knobs; and others that are tall and thin, or short and thick.

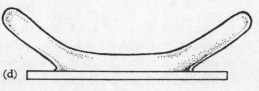
(d)

Throw separate knobs that could serve as handles if long enough, or act as lugs if short and solid (pl. 29); take a selection of these thrown handles or knobs and fix them to a cylindrical shape purely as an exercise, and perhaps add a lid that relates (fig. 31). As with the early clay exercises, throw contrasting forms and join two or more; even shape them by cutting if the form suggests such treatment.

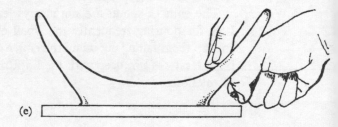
(e)

29 *Left* THROWING A CYLINDER
(a) Piece of clay centered on the wheel-head.
(b) Shape after inserting the thumb.
(c) Opening the clay, and shaping the inside base.
(d) Sides of the cylinder after first knuckling.
(e) Further thinning of the walls.
(f) The finished cylinder.

30 *Right* THROWING A BOWL
(a) Centred piece of clay.
(b) Shape after inserting the thumb.
(c) Shaping the inside.
(d) Beginning to shape the clay.
(e) Thinning the walls, showing the necessary outside support to retain a continuous curve on the inside.
(f) The finished bowl.

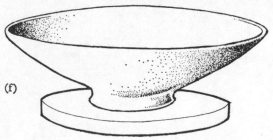
(f)

31

31 Applying thrown handles and knobs to a cylindrical shape, as an exercise in construction and relationships; by Jennifer Barnes, a student at the Central School.

All these can be developed in many ways that often suggest themselves as the clay grows on the wheel. Pulled handles and thrown spouts can be used as exercises related to varying forms where qualities of growth and tension can predominate. The technique of thrown and turned ware also offers a more precise approach to shape and proportion. (Turning is the trimming off of the excessive thickness of clay from the base of a pot while it is held in a chuck, or fixed with clay directly on the wheel-head.)

While even with the best instructors, students are taught to consider the practical points of throwing and making domestic ware, there are certain points that only experience can teach.

Firstly, there is the tendency to consider form more than function. This is particularly noticeable with all containers, be they bowls, vases, jugs, cups or even saucers. The bases are often not large enough, and are therefore unstable and impracticable. These articles are seldom seen in elevation, but only from above; therefore the consequent perspective must be taken into account when making the shape. Other common faults are handles that are too large, or so small that the fingers cannot fit easily between the handle and the body of the ware. Roll a coil of clay and fold it across the hand and you will soon discover the most practical shape for a handle. Many handles are far too narrow in width, making a firm grip difficult.

The ends of spouts are not always level or above the top of the teapot or jug, and the hole for pouring frequently too small or narrow. Often lids have very little or no flange to stop them falling out when the coffee or tea is being poured. The flange should generally be at least $1–1\frac{1}{2}$ in deep with the lid fitting as tightly as possible and having the minimum of tolerance.

29 Thrown shapes to be used as knobs or handles for exercise; see Fig. 31.

30 Stoneware jug. Student work.

31 Variations on a basic shape; by Ljubica Vasilyevitch.

32 Hand-built pot by Ljubica Vasilyevitch.

33 Vigorously thrown stoneware jars by Jennifer Knowland.

34 Tall stoneware bottle. Student work.

35 Stoneware bowl by Robin Welch. Author's collection.

36 Hand-shaped porcelain pot with matt glaze by Ruth Duckworth.

37 Hand-shaped porcelain bowl with iron decoration under a clear semi-matt glaze, by Gillian Lowndes. This piece shows an interesting development of form. Author's collection.

38 Elegant stoneware coffee-pot and milk jug by Lucie Rie. Author's collection.

39 Detail from a large mural by Antony Hollaway, A.R.C.A. Here standard commercial tiles have been broken and cut to varying sizes, and applied direct to the wall with mastic, the design having previously been drawn on the wall.

40 Section of large mural showing a map of the world, at Manchester Airport, designed and executed by Ceramic Consultants, using various forms of stoneware placing scrap, set in pre-cast concrete panels.

41 & 42 Ceramics in an architectural setting:
stoneware candle-holders in Coventry Cathedral
by Hans Coper.

43 Cement fondu and mosaic panels by Stephen Sykes for the Gethsemane Chapel at Coventry Cathedral.

44 Enlarged detail from Plate 43, showing the disciples asleep, from 'The Agony in the Garden'. A happy blending of two different materials. The central panel is of cement fondu, the surround of various forms of ceramic mosaic.

47 Hand-modelled chess-set in earthenware by Ann Wynn Reeves.

48 Tall vase, 24 in high, and large dishes, for an architectural project, from Kenneth Clark Pottery.

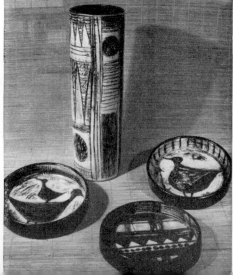

45 & 46 Two views of an unusually interesting exhibition held at University of London, Goldsmiths' College. The exhibition was entitled 'Prehistory to Picasso'; and included the work of students and contemporary potters. A stimulating experience, as many of the pieces were from the British Museum's most priceless collection, as well as from the Archaeological Museum, Cambridge, the Hanley, the London, and the Guildhall Museums.

49 & 50 Work by students from the Central School, London, showing a rich diversity of approach.

51 COLOUR IN STONEWARE AND EARTHENWARE
Sand cast, earthenware tile by the author.
Selection of coloured earthenware glaze tests.
Large stoneware dish by Robin Welch.
Earthenware mosaic panel by Ann Wynn Reeves.

52 Floor to ceiling wall mural in ceramic relief for small children's playroom in the new Civic Centre at Plymouth, Devon, by Ann Wynn Reeves. (Architects: Alan Ballantyne).

53 Designs from a range of individual flat dishes designed by Fletcher-Forbes-Gill, and made by Kenneth Clark Pottery. These were made by the thrown and turned method, and decorated with enamel colours on a white glaze.

54 Stoneware packaging jar designed by the author. Glazed with a matt white slip glaze, contrasting with the natural colour of the clay.

55 Wooden jars with ceramic lids by the author, showing the use of two different materials. The lids were made by jigger-and-jolly, and hand-decorated with rich coloured glazes.

56 Individual stew-pots, from a range of ware designed by the author and produced by Denby Pottery. The same methods and colours were used as for Plate 54.

57 Hand-made stoneware building tile, approximately 3 in thick, by Ruth Duckworth.

58 Ceramic sculpture of high-fired earthenware, made in four sections, and joined; standing 6 ft high; by Gordon Baldwin.

59 Recent stoneware developments in architectural ceramics by Ceramic Consultants in collaboration with the Shaw Hathenware Group of Companies. These include extruded pierced bricks, high-relief shadow tiles, large alphabet impressed panels, vari-coloured and shaped glazed wall tiles, a matt-white glazed barbecue, and a red-brown 4 ft 6 in diameter plant container.

60 Kitchen mural in a flat in Belgravia, by Ann Wynn Reeves, using dark blue, blue-green and lime green glazes.
61 Antony Hollaway working on a mural. He is rolling ceramic colours on to standard 6 × 6 in tiles, using a stencil technique.
62 Brian Southwell working on one of a series of large ceramic external panels. They were designed by John Farleigh and made by Kenneth Clark Pottery.

63 Thrown and turned stoneware shapes, set into the wall of a large office entrance; by Hans Coper.

64 Ceramic door push for plate glass door, by Nicholas Vergette.

65 Decorated porcelain shapes. An exercise in line, space and proportion.
66 Stoneware bowl by Gwen Hanssen, with a matt-grey mottled glaze having the quality of a black-
  bird's egg.
67 An exercise with incised and impressed patterns in small clay shapes.
68 Thrown jar with heavily incised decoration by Ann Wynn Reeves.

69 Hand-made stoneware bricks by Patricia O'Hare.

70 Structural exercise with coarse stoneware clay.

4 · Decoration · general principles

Decoration should be something that enriches and emphasizes form. It can be either structural or applied: structural when it results from the method of making, or from natural decorative effects inherent in the particular material, be it glaze or body; applied, when either patterns, symbols, shapes or ceramic materials have been added to the surface, by one or more of the many techniques of decoration, by hand or by machine.

Before discussing further the various forms decoration can take, we should examine and be fully conversant with the basic elements that are the vocabulary of decorative design. We may begin with a wide range of visual contrasts, which in some form or other will either predominate or be woven into the fabric of a design. Some of these are:

Areas of dark contrasted with areas of light
Large compared with small
Long lines against short
Sharp compared with rounded
Thin against thick
Curved compared with straight
Open shapes compared with enclosed
Fluid shapes contrasted with static
Textured surfaces opposed to smooth or plain

How few or how many of these elements are used depends on the discretion of the designer, and in no instance does the number of them have any bearing on the quality of the design. If we study the best decoration of any period we invariably find a predominating factor, be it a specific shape, arrangement of shapes, movement, weight of tone, or even colour, to which all other elements are subsidiary. As the playing of many instruments in an orchestra combine to form a single entity, so these elements relate to give a particular pot or form its complete personality.

32 Late Helladic Rhyton from Cyprus, about 1350 B.C. A good example of decoration, with a rich range of contrasts.

33

33 Susa Beaker 3500 B.C. Another excellent example of many contrasts, expressed with economy and clarity.

34 Boldly decorated Spanish dish of the fifteenth century.

33

34

35 Spanish fifteenth-century dish, showing a masterly control of pattern and related shapes.

36 Fig. 35, colours reversed to show the complete integration of background and design.

35

36

34

Everything must be carefully considered; when a shape is made it leaves a shape, or space (figs. 35, 36), which should also play its part in the composition. The essence of good decoration is that it should become so integrated with the form that we cannot dissociate pattern and shape.

When a repetitive geometric pattern is used, every consideration must be given to contrast, the important factor of interval, and vitality of execution; otherwise the result becomes dull and monotonous. Again the nature of decoration and the technique used must be in keeping with the character of the ware. An engraving or litho-print would be suitable for an earthenware or fine china teapot, but hardly appropriate if applied to a coiled pot. The way in which these basic formal values have been used (whatever the idiom or subject matter) will constitute the design's aesthetic merit.

It has already been said that the purpose of decoration is to enrich a form or surface with variations of texture, tone, line or colour, be they structural or applied. Structural decoration occurs mainly in hand-made wares as opposed to mechanical production: the richness of unsmoothed coils on a coiled Pueblo jar for example (pl. 11); or the patterns of texture on stoneware or earthenware pots caused by ash deposits in an open wood-fired kiln. And when a thrown shape has rich vigorous throwing rings on the surface, it may often seem superfluous and unnecessary to add any further decoration.

37 Vigorously decorated mug with Geometric pattern; from Athens, 2nd half of the eighth century B.C.

38 Decorated cup from late Geometric period, ninth to seventh centuries B.C.; made in Athens.

39 Elegant late Geometric-style mug from Corinth, of the eighth century B.C., with a simple but striking design.

In the past many applied patterns were developed from decoration that was originally structural, or from structural patterns in other natural materials such as basketry and marble. Some forms of structural decoration have been studied and intentionally used to add richness to our ceramics; the calculated use of metallic deposits in a stoneware body to combine with the glaze during firing, is a method of decoration successfully practised by some of our leading present-day studio potters, Lucie Rie amongst them (pl. 15).

Applied decoration is purely human in concept and application. Here man can observe or draw his own constructions, natural forms and patterns, to be assimilated in part or whole, and produce them as ideas or designs in the form of symbols or patterns to be used in an integrated way as decoration. It is thus an external element that is added to the ceramic surface or form.

Until recent times potters used accepted religious and social symbols and subjects from their culture to decorate their ware. Now there is no strong national vocabulary of decoration, but with modern communications we can become conversant with the best of the whole world, and its rich and varied traditions. As a result we often stand self-conscious and undecided, with only our personal vision and integrity to fall back on. With this, we must create a personal vocabulary from the wealth of our own visual experiences, combined with our imagination. Can this, we may ask ourselves, achieve the power and impetus inherent in the works of great past traditions, to which many people have contributed?

Drawing

With us drawing can play a very important part, in particular by helping us to explore and discover the world around us, while seeking to understand what we are looking at. If we gain knowledge from drawing we then have information we can use in many ways. We must observe, select, and record only those things which we consider to be important; and, though often difficult, we should regularly refresh and stimulate our visual vocabulary.

Basic design

In the past few years much emphasis has been placed on the teaching of 'basic design'. This is a method of exploring and experimenting in visual terms the basic principles of construction, movement, colour, tone, shape etc., unrelated to any specific subject matter. It can be vital and stimulating as an exercise to heighten sensibilities and deepen perception. However, unless it is practised in relation to personal visual knowledge and experience, it can become empty and lifeless.

Suggested exercises

We may now consider some practical exercises which may help to develop our sense of design and pattern making. Let us begin with the simplest of marks, a line. Read what Paul Klee has to say about it in *The Thinking Eye* or *Pedagogical Sketchbook*, observe, study and draw its endless qualities and variations, which are seen in every aspect of the world around us. With it we can express the whole range of contrasts mentioned earlier. When conversant with its qualities we can decorate a plain cylinder, sphere or flat surface in a

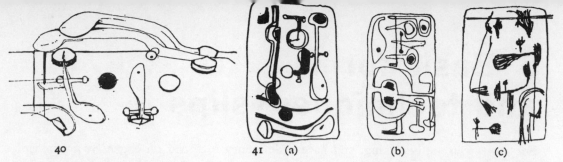

40

41   (a)   (b)   (c)

40 Detailed pen-drawing of section of a wood-wind instrument, by Eileen Nesbit, a 3rd-year student.
41 (a, b & c) Designs composed of elements taken from the drawing in fig. 40, showing the same subject treated in different ways.

hundred ways. For almost a decade, potters have been using and exploring this one element of design with an astonishing richness of effect, and a whole range of single or related marks and shapes can be treated in this way. The use of many elements does not necessarily produce a successful result. The more complex and rich the design, the greater must be the control and balance in order to avoid visual chaos and retain unity.

For those who have not practised some form of decoration from the beginning, the task of decorating a large shape can be, to say the least, inhibiting and frightening. By beginning with the decoration of small shapes, either hollow or solid, confidence will be gained; and as skill increases the size of the ware and decoration will grow together. How, you may well ask, does one apply knowledge contained in a drawing and use it for the decoration of ceramics? Obviously, to transfer a drawing direct to a curved ceramic surface is to ignore the third dimension; nevertheless a drawing as such, if carefully considered, can be used as a decorative unit on a form. Decoration must really be designed throughout and related to the form. By taking aspects of a drawing and applying the basic principles and contrasts, of line, mass, colour, movement etc., with the shape always in mind, some form of decoration should result. The drawing should primarily be seen as a composition of formal shapes and marks within a given area. Only when we appreciate these elements and see them objectively can we begin to use them as decoration.

A great help in making one aware of the shape of things, is to see them out of their normal context, and on a different scale. An example of this is shown, where a broken seed pod is carefully drawn to scale, squared up and then enlarged many times. In this way the shapes begin to assert themselves and take on a different dimension.

In all this, imagination with vision must play a leading role. We should not rely on a repetitive facility, expressing only a geometrically balanced type of pattern, which can become dull and boring.

Sir Kenneth Clark has said that the great change in art in the twentieth century was the change in emphasis to colour over form and sensation over idea; so, in the post-war years, has the element of assymetric balance predominated over that of a more mathematical or geometric order. This has been helped by the practise of basic design. But the principle is already present in natural phenomena, as we may rediscover through sound analytical drawing. This factor, together with the other basic principles should, then, greatly assist us in design work.

37

5 · Basic forms and techniques · slips

For those who are beginning, and have little money to spend on expensive equipment, many techniques are still available that require little more than basic clay and a kiln (complete with shelves) in which to fire the ware produced. Anyone studying the subject seriously hopes, in time, to sell his work; so from a production point of view a knowledge of certain industrial techniques can be of positive value.

Coiling

Coiling is a form of building, using long coils of clay approximately the thickness of one's thumb. For very large pots they will be relatively thicker. Rolling clay is best learnt from a skilled teacher. Each coil should form a complete circumference of the form before being moulded to the underneath coil. The clay should not be too hard, but of the same consistency as for throwing. Do not wet the coils in any way, and when a form is half-built allow to dry slightly in order to support further building; but while doing this keep the top edge covered and moist enough for continuing to build when the lower half is firm. It is advisable to use a somewhat open body for coiling; e.g., one third sand to two-thirds standard red clay.

Slab pots

Slab pots are made by joining together large flat pieces of rolled clay, to make simple forms. Little equipment is needed for making these pots, which are often severe and static in form. The method is simple, but the prepared slabs must be joined when they are firm, and before they become too hard. The clay should, therefore, be carefully watched after it has been rolled. When joining the slabs, do not apply quantities of surplus slip, as it will shrink unduly and cause cracking. To join slabs, lay one on the bench and wet the edge to be joined with a sponge. Then gently work the two areas of contact together, till a film of slip is created from the body clay, which causes the two surfaces to adhere firmly. Repeat this with the other slabs, and use a modelling tool to finish the edges. The form has neither the rhythm nor the flow of a thrown or coiled shape, which must be taken into consideration when it is being decorated. Slabbing, however, is not restricted to rectangular forms, but can be used successfully in building large curved shapes.

Jigger and jolly

Another technique that could be exploited more fully than it is today is that of jigger-and-jollying. Making ware on a jigger and jolly entails the use of a power wheel with cup-head or chuck, into which the moulds are placed. The wheel also needs a jolly-arm attachment for holding the template which shapes the back of the dish.

Here, where a number of identical moulds are produced, each one can be incised with an individual pattern (pl. 26), thus giving a wide range of designs when the ware is made in only limited quantities. The articles are then individually decorated or glazed.

42 Drawings of widely varying slab-built forms.

In Scandinavia this technique, and many others, are practised by studio potters working for the large manufacturers on their premises, with all the factories' resources and skills to assist them in their work. How, you may rightly say, can we hope to compete unless we enjoy similar conditions?

Plaques

These can be made in several ways, either individually or by using a plaster recess mould from a clay original. From the mould, clay pressings may be taken and each piece decorated in a variety of colours or methods. Sprigging is the same technique on a much smaller scale. Here, however, the clay is lifted from the mould and fixed to a clay article with a thin film of slip. Contrasting coloured clays can be used in this way.

Pressed dishes

The making of pressed dishes has already been discussed in Chapter 3, but when made they can be decorated in the damp clay state, or bone dry, biscuited, or glazed. When the clay is soft, patterns may be rolled into the clay to give a shallow, textured surface. If this is later covered with a coloured transparent glaze, the varying thickness due to the unevenness of the surface produces an attractive variation in tone, giving definition to the pattern. Sgraffito, wax resist, incising, slip trailing (see page 50) and practically every other decorative technique can be used on pressed dishes.

Press moulds

A press mould is a two-piece mould. Each half is lined with a thick layer of plastic clay and the two pieces of mould pressed firmly together, forcing the leading edges of the clay to adhere. The mould is then gently parted, the whole article taken out, and any seams filled with clay and smoothed with a modelling tool.

When the production of a limited number of a very simple shape is planned, this method of making can be most satisfactory. When the main form has hardened, further modelling may be applied. Forms made from glazed earthenware are greatly enhanced by some form of decoration.

Folded clay

Clay is rolled in the same way as for dishes, after which it is cut and shaped in a sculptural manner (fig. 6). As the shape hardens, extra clay can be added if desired. According to form and subject, decoration can be applied with brush and pigment or with glaze when fired.

Slips

There are two main types of slip. The first is clay mixed with water to various degrees of fluidity; it is used for slip trailing and decorating, when either the natural colour of the clay may be exploited or colouring agents added. The second is casting-slip, or clay having a liquid state mainly induced by the addition of certain chemicals called deflocculents, together with a very small quantity of water.

SLIP CASTING The technique of slip casting is as follows. Fill a hollow plaster mould with slip of the correct consistency. Where the slip makes contact with the plaster surface, some of the moisture is absorbed by the mould, giving a firm layer, while the mould is still full of liquid clay. The longer the slip remains in the mould, the thicker the layer becomes. When the required thickness has been achieved – which can be seen at the top edge of the mould – the surplus slip is poured out and drained from the mould. After some twenty to thirty minutes, the clay shape is firm enough to stand alone, and the mould is parted and the shape withdrawn. When almost dry, the shape is trimmed and sponged in readiness for biscuit firing.

This is a method of production which could be used by many more small workshops, as well as by studio potters. The advantage of this technique is that, once a good shape or model has been made, it can then be moulded and many more identical articles be produced mechanically. This method is particularly advocated when clay figures or animals are to be produced; which may then be individually decorated using various techniques.

The main cost in making ware produced by slip casting is in the initial production of the master, and block moulds; the subsequent cost of making and decorating being relatively small. Where an industrial technique is used, it should be regarded as a means to an end. There is obviously no point in producing ware that is more easily or better made in the industry, but we must adapt and use industry's techniques and machines for our own ends. This approach was very evident in the work of some of the early Staffordshire potters, such as Whieldon and Astbury, who certainly made the machine serve them. The vitality and richness of their work is evidence of their imaginative use of newly developed methods.

Preparing slip

When preparing a slip, weigh out the necessary quantity of water, then heat some of this in order to dissolve the deflocculents (described below) more easily. Add this to the remaining water and then slowly stir in the dry ingredients till all have been added. The result will generally be too solid, but after sieving twice through a 100-mesh sieve and leaving to stand for at least twenty-four hours, it should be sufficiently fluid and suitable for use. In making a slip that contains coarse materials, such as grog or sand, either sieve through a very coarse mesh or add the sand after the other materials have been prepared and sieved.

SLIP FOR CASTING The principle of making casting slip is to create a liquid clay with the minimum water content, but the right degree of flow. The less water present, the smaller the shrinkage of the cast article. Where moist throwing clay contains 22% by weight of water, and slip for trailing (see page 43) some 60%, casting slip contains only 40 to 45% of water. This is made possible by the addition of small quantities of certain chemicals called electrolytes. The percentage of these present depends mainly on the degree of plasticity of the clay. The acids and acid salts present in clay have the effect of making its particles coagulate and form a gel; and this is known as flocculation.

When small amounts of certain chemicals such as soda ash and water glass are added, the clay particles are deflocculated, as the process is called, and the slip becomes more fluid. The general rule when making casting slips is to add approximately ·3% of sodium silicate, ·3% of soda ash, and 40% water by weight, to the mixture. The old saying is 'the greater the pint weight the better the slip' as long as it is sufficiently fluid. This should never be less than 32 oz to the pint.

The two main electrolytes, or deflocculents, as they are called, sodium silicate and soda ash, have different properties:

Sodium silicate is a mixture of sodium oxide and silica, originally fritted (page 57), then dissolved in water, with heat and pressure. It is available in various degrees of concentration and is defined as degrees Twaddle (°T). There is 140°T which contains 45% of water and is a thick sticky liquid, while 100°T is a thinner liquid containing 60% water; these are used in the more plastic bodies. Another, of 75°T is a thinnish solution and is more suitable for less plastic porcelain and china clay slips.

Sodium silicate gives more fluidity than soda ash, and consequently a more broken, stringy effect, like syrup, while being drained from the mould. It also gives harder casts than soda ash, since it tends to adhere to the mould, and when dry is liable to be brittle and break when being fettled and sponged.

Soda ash is a light, white powder, which must be kept in a dry, airtight container, as it easily absorbs moisture, changing to sodium bicarbonate which has the opposite effect to that required (i.e., it coagulates the slip). Soda ash drains better than sodium silicate, but gives soft flabby casts which tend to sag away from the mould, and consequently prevent drying. With more plastic clays, soda ash gives a more rapid cast, though the slip itself is less fluid. It also gives a high surface tension, which causes the slip to break into globules when being poured, thus trapping small air bubbles in the clay. These air bubbles later cause damage to the ware in the form of pinholing, which becomes more apparent when the ware is glazed.

To obtain the best results, a happy balance of both deflocculents is desirable. These proportions will vary according to the composition of the clay. The more plastic the clay, the greater should be the proportion of soda ash; and conversely, the less plastic the clay, the greater the proportion of sodium silicate. This particularly applies to coarse clays containing grog, clays containing no ball clay, and plastic fire clay.

When storing casting slip for a time, it will be found that it tends to flocculate if it contains only just enough alkali to bring the mix to the maximum state of deflocculation; but if an excess is present, this will not occur. If, however, too great an excess of alkali is added, the slip becomes thick, and solid, and this is only reversed by the addition of more clay and the correct percentage of water.

Slip should not be used immediately after preparation, but, if possible, mixed with a blunger for several hours, and then allowed to stand for at least twenty-four hours, in order to allow complete combination and chemical action to take place. It should, however, be mixed again before use.

If you do not possess a mechanical mixer, but make smaller quantities of slip in a bucket or large metal container, stir with a stick or your hand in such a way that you do not beat air into the slip. Always keep the container covered, as the water content will evaporate, and the carbon dioxide in the air will cause a skin to form on the surface of the slip. This skin, if stirred into the mixture, can later give brownish patches to the sides of the ware.

Keep a separate container for all the fettlings and unsuccessful casts, which should be soaked and then sieved. A little more deflocculent should be added if necessary, as some of this, in combination with the water, is absorbed into the mould at each casting.

If slip goes sludgy, like junket, after standing for a while, in the next batch reduce the soda ash content, and increase the sodium silicate. Alternatively, by adding ·2 to ·5 % of barium carbonate, the soluble salts in the clay will be changed to insoluble salts, restoring the balance of the slip; but barium salts should be used with great care as they are usually more troublesome than helpful.

The more plastic the clay, the longer and more difficult the cast, as the plasticity prevents easy absorption of the water. I have known some industrial slips to remain in the moulds for a matter of hours, due to plasticity, and, on the other hand, a non-plastic porcelain slip to cast up in a matter of seconds.

When pouring the slip into the mould, where possible let it run slowly in from the edge, or direct the flow to the base of the mould. Wherever the slip makes impact with the mould with too great a velocity, there is a concentration of the non-plastic fluxes in the body which, in the biscuit firing, gives excessive vitrification at this point, reducing porosity and giving bald patches on glazing; this is commonly known as 'flashing'.

The length of time that the slip should remain in the mould will depend on the thickness required, and this can easily be seen if the slip is regularly topped up and not allowed to sink. The increasing thickness of the cast can be seen by slightly tilting the mould to reveal the highest edge of the cast on the 'spare' or top edge (fig. 43). If a mould is too dry, it can cause the article to crack, unless taken out soon after the slip has been drained. On the

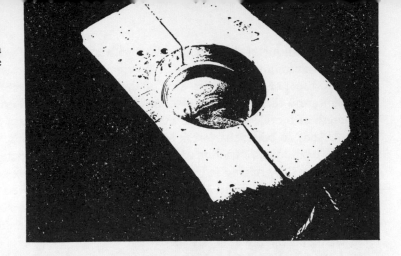

43 Tilting a mould when casting to check the thickness of the cast.

other hand, if the mould has been used several times previously on the same day, a longer period will be necessary for casting, and the article will need to remain a considerable time in the mould in order to dry sufficiently. Sagging or collapsing of articles in the mould while draining, can be caused by too damp a mould, and too violent an emptying of the slip, creating a vacuum which draws the cast clay away from the sides of the mould.

Do not pour the slip in too slowly, as it may make circular lines in the ware, especially if the mould is very dry.

A good basis for a prepared slip is to start with approximately 50% of ball clay and varying quantities of felspar or china stone, china clay and flint. For example: Ball clay 50%, Felspar 20%, China clay 20% and Flint 10%.

SLIP FOR DECORATING AND TRAILING   This can be prepared from either a standard powdered body or from dried-out, unfired pots, if available, or from a recipe of pottery materials, with ball clay as the main constituent.

For the first, take a given quantity of water in a wide, shallow container, slowly sprinkle the powdered clay on the surface and allow to sink. Continue until the suspension is saturated. Allow to stand, and then sieve through an 80- or 100-mesh sieve.

For the second, break up the dry pots into small pieces (the size of pigeons' eggs or slightly larger) and put these into a wide bowl. Just cover with water, do not disturb or mix, and wait for approximately 40 to 60 minutes until the clay particles have completely disintegrated. Gently pour off the surplus water and sieve the mixture in the usual way. There should be no hard lumps left in the bowl, provided the clay was bone dry to start with.

For the third method, weigh out your ingredients and treat in the same way as for a powdered body. If the ball clay is coarse and unprepared, dry out and break up, treating it at first as in the second method, and then adding the other ingredients.

When making slip it is advisable to use a clay similar in type to the article that is being slipped or decorated. Difficulties may arise when the article is made in too coarse or grogged amixture and where the shrinkage of the applied slip is consequently greater than that of the article.

43

As the technique of decoration is dealt with elsewhere, we will only deal here with the necessary minimum of equipment. If no standard slip trailer is available, make a funnel from newspaper or brown paper. Tear off the point, fold from the filling end as with a toothpaste tube, and then gently squeeze. Another method is to insert a quill into a cork fitted to a length of bicycle tube. Fill in the same way, fold over, and commence trailing.

One cannot do better than work on the old principle of black, white and halftone when using this technique, restricting oneself to the use of white, red and black slip. A great deal can be achieved by mixing red and white slip in various proportions and then using black slip as an accent or contrast. Black slip should be made from red clay with the addition of between 8 and 10%, not more, of manganese oxide, and prepared in the dry state, with the slip made in the usual way. Too much manganese will fuse the slip – and prevent the glaze from taking on the biscuited article.

Do not apply the slip too thinly or it may be dissolved by the glaze in firing. However if controlled, this fact can be used to advantage as a decorative technique.

44 An improvised slip trailer, made from rolled and folded paper.
45 Two standard slip trailers from retailers.
46 Slip trailer made from a quill, cork, and section of a cycle tube.

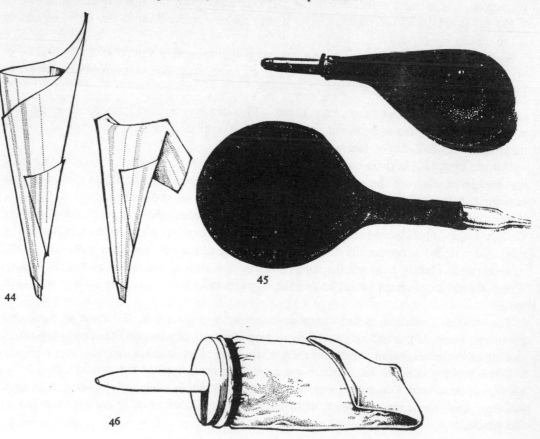

44

45

46

6 · Ceramic colours and decorative methods

In this chapter, the word decoration will be used in its broadest sense, when used either on purely functional wares, or for a purely decorative effect.

We can begin with the basic metallic oxides, and discuss some of their possible uses:

Ferric or iron oxide – Fe_2O_3

A universal colouring pigment staining all red clays. In red clay slip, it is used for many decorative techniques, from trailing and coating, to decorative brushwork, and as a surface for sgraffito.

When some 6% of iron oxide is used in a transparent glaze, it gives a rich, deep, honey colour (pl. 82). This is particularly effective over impressed decoration, or on broken surfaces giving contrasts of tone from the varying densities of colour. If the pigment is used with a brush or sponge, either under, or over a transparent lead-based glaze, it is necessary to apply a sufficient weight of colour to prevent it being dissolved by the glaze; it is, however, more stable in a leadless glaze. Iron oxide gives rich red-browns when used on an opaque white glaze, but should not be applied too thickly; when overfired on this glaze, the pigment tends to break up and lose definition. Small quantities of up to 2% of ferric oxide added to a stoneware glaze give pale blues or greens, in a reduction firing, described on page 68. As the quantity is increased to 10%, it gives colours from greenish-brown to black, or rust red if a 10% iron glaze is applied thinly. This oxide is sometimes used with other oxides, in making black glazes. Very rich effects are obtained where it is mixed with copper oxide, and when used in various forms of decoration.

Copper oxide – CuO

A black metallic powder with a wide range of uses. It is little used in industry, because of its high solubility in the glaze, giving running faults, and excessive volatility. It gives a soft green when applied thinly as decoration, and is more effective for work with semi-matt or opaque glazes. When the pigment is applied too heavily it over-saturates the glaze, giving a black, matt, crystalline, metallic surface; a quality sometimes intentionally induced.

As a pigment used alone, mixed with iron oxide, or used to give a metallic glaze alongside an opaque white glaze, it produces a soft, dark green flush at the edges. In much the same way copper can be mixed with wax to make a resist (described on page 50). The mixture is used hot when decorating, and the article then glazed with an opaque white glaze, by pouring. This technique was used a great deal by Picasso in his early experiments with ceramics.

All the other basic metallic pigments when mixed individually with copper give suitable colours for decoration, as well as forming excellent combinations for coloured glazes.

Copper oxide is the pigment used for many lovely transparent green glazes, having a lead base. These can be made successfully with up to 4% of oxide. While a rich green is obtained with copper only, a wide range of beautiful colours are possible by combining it in various proportions with yellow stains, or with iron oxide. When 4% copper oxide and 2% iron oxide are added to a transparent glaze, this can be applied to a buff or white clay body, and may act as a background for decoration with prepared black pigments. By adding up to 3% of copper to an alkaline glaze with a high silica content, a range of turquoise blues to greens can be obtained. The best results are obtained by using an unfritted alkali, but after firing they tend to devitrify, and a white scum will form on the surface of the glaze.

Turquoise glazes are best used on fairly flat surfaces, and then mainly for their richness as decoration. These glazes tend to flow easily from the more vertical surfaces, due to the small amount of alumina that they can contain. Turquoise colours can be obtained by firing at stoneware temperatures, using copper oxide and unfritted alkalies, together with silica.

In an oxidized stoneware firing, a pleasant green is obtained with small quantities of oxide; in a reduction firing, under certain conditions, red colours can be achieved. Copper carbonate – $CuCO_3$ – being green in the raw state, is often used for decoration, because it gives a good indication of what the strength and intensity of the fired colour will be.

Cobalt oxide – CoO

A strong, stable, metallic oxide, giving pale blue to black, according to the quantity or the type of glaze used. As little as ·25%, in an opaque white earthenware glaze, gives a definite blue. It is the basis for most blue glazes, but is seldom used alone because of its primary intensity. It is best mixed with a little copper or manganese, and it is contained in many black glazes. When a very small quantity is finely ground with antimoniate of lead, or with yellow glaze stain, a very beautiful grey-green can be obtained for use in majolica painting. A black pigment made with cobalt and manganese can give brilliant effects when used in combination with turquoise glazes. Cobalt oxide has a fluxing effect on glazes when used in quantity; this should not exceed 10% and, at this point, it gives a dark, blue-black glaze. Very rich, dark colours can be achieved in oxidized stoneware glazes by mixing with iron oxide. Good results are possible when the following glaze is applied to raw stoneware clay and then fired:

Felspar	52%			
Whiting	22%	+	Cobalt oxide	8%
Flint	2%		Iron oxide	2%
Plastic clay	24%			

FIRE TO 1250°C–1280°C

In a medium oxidized stoneware glaze 8% cobalt oxide plus 4% iron oxide gives a matt blue with iron, breaking to a matt grey.

Manganese oxide, or dioxide, as commonly used – MnO₂

A brownish-black powder giving pale mauve to brown, when small quantities are added to lead glazes, and black when 10% is used. In leadless glazes it gives a purple colour, but becomes unstable over 1100°C. Most black slips and glazes contain a predominance of manganese oxide with the addition of cobalt or copper or iron oxide. The manganese, when used alone, or when mixed with cobalt or copper oxide, is a traditional colour for majolica decoration. In stoneware glazes it gives a pale lavender to mushroom-grey, according to the recipe.

46

Chromium oxide – Cr_2O_3

This is rather a dull green powder, with refractory qualities when used in glazes. In lead glazes it gives a wide range of colours, from sharp greenish-yellow, to deep greens and brown, depending on the quantity added. A bright yellow chartreuse colour can be obtained in a lead glaze, with as little as ·3% of chrome. When 2–3% is used in slips, it gives a range of soft grey-greens. Great care should be taken when using this pigment on or near glazes containing tin oxide and lime, as it gives a violent pink reaction. Many under-glaze blacks are prepared from chrome, so they should also be kept away from a tin and lime glaze. Chrome is used to make many commercial maroon glazes and stains, which can be useful if mixed or blended with other colours and glazes, providing that the above precautions are born in mind.

Tin oxide – SnO_2

A white powder, which has been used for many centuries for making opaque white glazes, by adding between 8 and 10% to a transparent glaze. Tin does not dissolve, but remains in suspension in a glaze, and the quantity used can vary considerably, according to the glaze composition. As an example, a glaze made from unfritted raw lead can comfortably carry up to 20% of tin oxide, which naturally allows it to be applied thinly, and still retain maximum opacity. Throughout the history of majolica glazes, these have been used mainly as white backgrounds, to be richly decorated with the standard oxides already mentioned. Unless a wealth of decoration is applied, the large white areas can appear cold and overpowering, making the decoration look thin and isolated. I am sure that this is one reason why most Italian, French, Spanish and Dutch majolica articles were so lavishly decorated.

Another technique much used in this past decade has been to apply oxides to raw clay, or to biscuit, and then apply and fire a tin glaze. The coloured pigments permeate and stain the glaze, giving rich patterns of colour, which are virtually areas of coloured glaze, or glazes. This technique is often combined with various forms of wax resist and sgraffito, after the glaze is applied, as well as further application of different coloured glazes to specific areas. In this way, a rich sense of integrated, rather than applied, pattern is achieved (pl. 74). There are now several alternative opacifiers, such as the zircon group, and zinc, if used in the correct proportions. Though expensive, tin is still the most satisfactory.

An extremely decorative use for tin glaze is to apply it to a transparent glazed and fired terra-cotta dish or pot. When dry, a design can be scratched through to the clear glaze and the article fired. According to how thickly the glaze was applied, a rich broken textured design can result, giving at the same time, strong tonal contrasts when used in this way on a transparent glaze containing 6% of iron oxide. It is always advisable to add a little gum to the second (tin) glaze, to prevent excessive chipping from handling when dry. Remember, however, that most gums have a deflocculating effect, so add the gum to the dry glaze, and then add the necessary water.

When decorating large surfaces, a combined use of opaque-white, coloured-transparent, and matt glazes are well worth considering. All this naturally requires a great deal of experience, to achieve controlled results.

Antimoniate of lead and yellow glaze stains

These yellows can be used for various forms of decoration, but are seldom used alone on a surface or form, as they contribute insufficient weight of tone. Their use, however, for colouring glazes, is endless, but here again the addition of a little of some other stain or colouring pigment gives the most satisfactory results. An excellent greenish-yellow can be obtained by adding 5 % yellow, 2 % tin oxide and ·5 % copper oxide to a basic transparent glaze. However, the mixing of colours and the making of coloured glazes will be discussed more fully in the next chapter.

If applying yellow thickly as decoration, some form of lead as a flux should be added to counteract dryness and bubbling in firing, which will also occur if a yellow glaze is applied too thickly. Most earthenware yellows are unstable when fired above 1100°C. A clear glaze applied over the yellow stain, helps to stabilize the colour, even at a higher temperature. Because of its dryness, antimoniate of lead is not able to stain an opaque glaze, when used under it, and is only suitable for earthenware.

The preceding paragraphs have shown some of the ways in which I have used various pigments, but there are still endless possibilities for their further use and development.

Mention should be made of other types of colour that can be used to give added breadth to ceramics generally, including most of the commercial colour ranges of glaze stains, under-glaze colours, body stains, enamel colours and lustres. So much will depend on the ways in which these are used; and, because the colours are used for industrial reproduction, they are of necessity individually uniform and often lacking in richness. Should the ceramist, however, explore their possibilites in a completely different context the results, to say the least, can be exciting.

I well remember visiting a factory in Stoke-on-Trent and being shown some particularly attractive, decorated tea-ware that was a best seller, and had been for some years. The proprietors' competitors had tried to copy it as a result, but without success; all that had happened was that, by mistake, a piece of ware with an all-over enamel engraved print had overfired, and the colour fused well into the glaze, giving a now delightful, soft, textured result. This was then repeated intentionally and as a consequence became a great success commercially.

Having discussed some decorative uses of basic colouring oxides, we may now consider a wider range of techniques, which combine these and other ceramic materials.

To begin with just clay, there have, in recent years, been many developments of the tile technique. From being nothing more than a necessity for lavatories and bathrooms, it has developed into a rich source of architectural decoration and this includes brilliantly-coloured mosaics, hand-made tiles and panels, let into walls as murals, both large and small.

When the ceramic pieces are large and heavy, they can be screwed into the wall, as well as being set in the usual way with sand and cement; the holes for the screws can blend with the design, and later be filled with coloured pointing, or small glazed plugs that match the surround glaze colour (fig. 47). When working on external walls, the local District Surveyor will have some definite views on fixing.

71 Earthenware dish in pink clay, with a thin tin glaze. Made from an incised mould designed by Picasso. Nommie Durell collection.

72 A composition of tiles with rolled and pressed patterns, decorated with metallic oxides and covered with a majolica glaze; by a student.

73 Two tiles decorated in the sgraffito glaze-on-glaze technique by Simon Clark, aged 5. Note the similar use of sun, figure and plants as shown in Plate 71.

74 Large pressed dish decorated with wax resist, oxides and majolica glaze. By Ann Wynn Reeves.

75 Hand-built unglazed oxidized stoneware lamp bases, 24 in high, from Kenneth Clark Pottery.

76 Owl jug, decorated in blue and black on a white glaze. Made by the Madoura Pottery, Vallauris, after the original by Picasso. Author's collection.

77 Unglazed porcelain birds by Ann Wynn Reeves.

78 Decorated paper cylinders, designs for children's mugs. By Ann Wynn Reeves. A good method of developing ideas for decoration.

79 Detail of large earthenware wall mosaic by Nicholas Vergette for the Syracuse Cathedral Baptistry, U.S.A.

80 Two earthenware dishes from designs by Lurcat; from the collection of Mr and Mrs Alan Ballantyne.

81 Majolica jar by Alan Caiger-Smith.
    Earthenware vases by Ann Wynn Reeves.
    Dish decorated by Brian Southwell, using coloured glaze, wax resist and majolica.

82 Red earthenware plate by the author. Earthenware beakers, shapes designed by Gordon Baldwin.

83 Slip decorated dish, in red, white and black, by Sophia Gray, aged 9. This shows a child's free
and uninhibited use of the medium, so essential to good slipware. Collection Nicolete Gray.

84 & 85 Two large slip-decorated chargers by William Newland. They both show his masterly hand-
    ling of the slip and his ability to exploit fully its fluid quality.

86 Majolica bowl with area of matt-yellow, and copper pigment; by Picard, the French potter.
    Author's collection.

87 Majolica bowl with resist decoration, using copper oxide mixed with wax. Made by Madoura
    Pottery, Vallauris, after the original by Picasso. Author's collection.

88 Stoneware dish, 24 in, with brushed iron decoration, by Eileen Nisbet.

89 Brush-drawing by Eileen Nisbet.

90 Exercises in the use of brushwork and wash by Eileen Nisbet, a student.

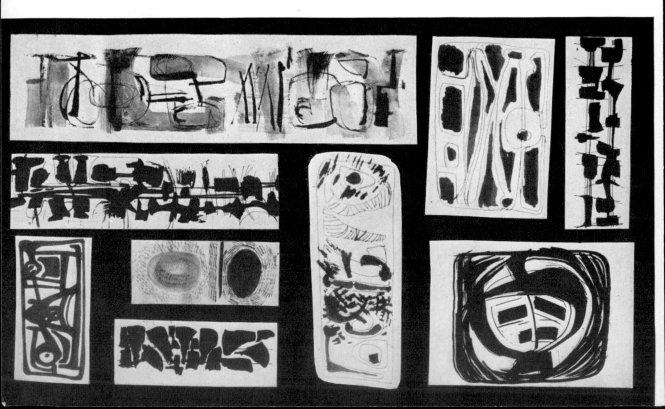

Once the method of fixing has been agreed, there is no limit to the form the ceramic can take. I have seen large thrown stoneware discs set into a wall (pl. 63), and again another wall covered with a sea of dark, textured, red-black stoneware units. Decorated dishes, tiles, clay shapes and richly glazed ceramic stones, have all been set in plaster or cement to enrich wall surfaces. In certain instances where cost has been the deciding factor, large murals have been executed using hand-cut coloured commercial tiles, giving the effect of giant mosaics. These have been applied direct with standard tile adhesives (pl. 39). High fired, vitrified ceramic scrap has been used, set in 2 × 3 ft pre-cast concrete slabs, to give a relief surface design to a large wall at one of our new airports (pl. 40).

Ceramists should visit building sites, and become thoroughly conversant with the many methods and techniques of fixing both pre-cast slabs and other forms of ceramic. This would assist the planning of projects, and avoid having to re-make pieces which later proved to be impractical, or too expensive to fix. Ingenuity, forethought and resourcefulness in making, glazing, and firing, can often increase narrow profit margins.

Unfired clay has often been mixed with non-ceramic materials. These can include various grades of cork that fire away, giving a distinct porous quality to the clay; which also makes it lighter, and less dense, and, in some cases, burns a red clay to a rich blue-black colour in a reducing atmosphere. Chaff, or other vegetable matter can be equally effective. Particles of certain metallic oxides can be mixed in a stoneware body, to give a speckly texture to the surface when the glaze has been applied and fired. This is equally true for certain sands in stoneware bodies, in a reducing firing. Crisp, semi-dry turnings from the potter's wheel, can be stuck to the surface of the ceramic by first applying a coating of slip. Again, coarse or fine grog can be mixed with slip and applied to the unfired clay, then fired to earthenware or stoneware temperatures, and either glazed, or left in the vitrified state.

Though the traditional methods of glazing are dipping, pouring and spraying, for decorative purposes glaze can be applied with a brush or spoon, and in many cases a slip trailer can be used for greater control.

In the field of glazes and glazing, the possibilities are limitless. Where it has not been possible to achieve a sufficiently textured surface for a project, this can be done by applying and firing to the biscuit surface, a mixture of coarse grog and a quantity of frit or glaze. The flux should be sufficient to create adhesion at the required temperature, without causing the mass to melt and flow. Pigments or glazes can then be applied and fired in the usual way. There was a time when anything but a fine, smooth, well-matured, glazed surface was viewed with horror by many people. One can, however, only assess and judge the final result, decide whether it achieves its purpose, and whether the purpose was well served by ceramics.

Many experiments and projects have been carried out using stained glass with ceramic. It can be either broken into small pieces and applied thickly to an area, or, if the surface is flat, shapes, or squares of glass can be arranged on it and then fired. Some of the difficulties are the varying melting points (900–1100°C) of the different colours, the fact that some change colour in firing or in contact with the ceramic (particularly the reds), and that most of the soda-glass blues will scum and devitrify after firing. The advantages are thick, clear, brilliant colours not so easily obtained with ceramic frits, or transparent glazes.

Other very beautiful effects have been achieved by placing a large square (or other shapes) of stained glass on a white commercial tile, then arranging a pattern of small pieces on top, and allowing the superimposed pieces to melt and settle into the underglass, giving a very lovely mosaic effect. There are several variations of this technique, but great discretion is needed in the use of colours, the placing of the pieces and control of the firing. Needless to say, the price of some stained glass makes it an extremely expensive technique.

The decorative use of slip

Slip trailing is the controlled application of liquid clay to a moist clay surface, by using a slip trailer or rubber bag to which is attached a tapered nozzle for directing the flow of the slip (figs. 44–46).

The first essential is to explore and master the full possibilities of this medium. There is no better beginning than to roll out a slab of clay, cover it with a coating of liquid red or white slip and, with a trailer full of a contrasting colour, experiment with shapes, lines, and patterns (figs. 48, 49). (Remembering all the qualities of contrast mentioned in Chapter 4, this is a very direct medium in which to practise the basic elements of design.) From this you can proceed by pouring larger areas of contrasting coloured slip across a clay dish in a supporting mould to give the impression of collage. Then after an initial coating has been applied to an area it can be sponged away and another colour introduced. It is advisable to think well before you begin, in order to clarify the image you wish to express in relation to the particular shape.

The essential character of slip is one of spontaneity and boldness. The slip should flow freely and steadily, and the result should never be laboured (pls. 84, 85).

These exercises should be done time and again, until a directness and confidence is achieved. If several dishes or slabs are prepared, then a design can progress and develop, and the best be kept.

Wax resist

Wax resist is, basically, wax applied to a surface in a hot liquid form, allowed to harden and then covered with a fluid slip or glaze. This is repelled by the waxed areas, but adheres to untreated surfaces. Cold liquid resists are also available.

It can be used in a variety of ways. Rubbing dry clay with a wax candle, and then brushing areas with metallic pigments to give a broken-textured, coloured surface when the article is fired and glazed, is an interesting but little used technique (pl. 25). One of the most common methods is to brush hot wax onto the raw clay or biscuit, before glazing, in order to achieve a contrast in colour between the body of the article, and the glaze later applied. This is obviously more suitable for stoneware, as the areas resisted become vitrified and therefore non-porous. This, to some extent, is overcome in the case of earthenware, when

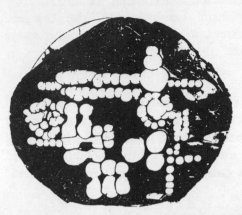

48 & 49 Slip trailing exercises with black and white Slip.

a metallic pigment is mixed with the wax, which fires away leaving the pigment, which then fuses to the body in firing, reducing the porosity of the surface, but no longer showing the colour of the clay body (pl. 87).

This method can be taken a stage further to give contrasts between two different glazes, but it often involves the cost of a third firing. It can be carried out in one glaze firing, but great skill is necessary in applying the second coat of glaze, when the first has not already been fired. Several forms of wax can be used when preparing a resist. The final result should give a fairly hard surface, so that the thick glaze does not adhere, but not so hard that the wax flakes from the ware before the pigment or glaze is applied. If, on the other hand, the wax is too soft, it will not cleanly resist the glaze. One method of avoiding this is to melt candle-grease, which is rather hard, with a small amount of beeswax, which has a softening, resilient effect.

Perhaps the most common single resist is paraffin wax melted with paraffin, and applied with either a sable or a camel-hair mop brush, according to the required result.

Brushwork

The use of brushwork in ceramic decoration during the past twenty years has passed through difficult and often self-conscious stages. We can not ignore the influence of Chinese and Japanese brushwork, but if we make any contribution in this medium we require something more than facility. Because of this association, it is difficult to use a brush purely as a means, rather than as an end, in itself. A useful antedote to too many Chinese brushes would be to use an old shaving brush, or hog's-hair brush, and so discover and use brush marks, other than those of the accepted oriental symbol. One will thus become aware of stippling (fine broken textures), dragging, and the qualities of dry brush techniques which, though different, are perfectly valid when used with perception (pl. 90).

Sponging

Sponging is the applying with a moist sponge of a colouring oxide in the wet state to ceramics, as a form of decoration. Slip and glaze can also be applied in this way, but less successfully. It is a simple, but effective and direct method of decoration, handled superbly by the majolica painters of the eighteenth century Bristol, Lambeth and Chelsea chargers. It was most commonly used as patterning for trees, or for an all-over pattern using manganese, copper, and cobalt oxides on a tin glaze.

Silhouette and cut-out

For those who are diffident concerning their ability as draughtsmen, a beginning to decoration can be made through the application of cut or torn shapes of paper to a damp clay surface. Here the shapes can be considered and arranged to form the required relationships, and then a coating of slip or brushed pigments applied. The paper is then carefully removed when the slip or pigment is dry. This idea can be varied and developed for other ceramic media, even glazes.

Ceramic mosaic

When a range of suitable coloured earthenware glazes has been developed, these can be applied to standard white commercial tiles, fired, and then cut in strips with a tile cutter. These strips are then cut with tile pincers, into tessera of required size, and are used for mosaics in the usual way. While this is rather a slow and laborious task, it does give maximum freedom of choice of colour, and size of the tessera. It is still a quicker and more satisfactory method than making, firing and glazing your own mosaic.

When sufficient pieces have been prepared, they should be arranged on a board with temporary wooden strip sides, equivalent in size to the surface that will be finally covered with the mosaic design. When this is complete, square sheets or strips of gummed paper are wetted, applied to the face of the mosaic and allowed to dry. The mosaic and paper can then be removed safely, area by area, and placed on the prepared wall or panel. When the mosaic has set firmly in the mastic, the paper is again moistened and peeled off, and the spaces between the mosaic filled with a white or coloured pointing. Sometimes wide strips of cellotape can be used, instead of the gummed paper, for transfering the areas o mosaic.

Finally, it is well to remember that some potters have built their reputation on the use of an extremely limited range of materials and colours, while others have worked with a rich variety of techniques.

7 · Glazing

To many people who found chemistry at school a difficult subject, the thought of acquiring at least a working knowledge of ceramic chemistry, is somewhat alarming. However, unless one understands the basic principles of glaze formulae and proportions, the field of experiment so vital to the artist-potter will be greatly restricted and he will have to rely on other people's glaze recipes, or carry out a series of purely empirical experiments on a trial or error basis.

Recently, several very good books of great clarity and breadth, have been written on this particular branch of ceramics. Here, we intend to deal only with the basic principles, and to suggest, in the light of experience, directions for further experiment.

It has already been noted that some 75% of the composition of rocks forming the earth's crust, to a depth of ten miles, are composed of aluminium oxide (Al_2O_3) and silica (SiO_2) in varying proportions. As most clays were derived from the decomposition of rocks, it is not surprising to learn that alumina and silica together make up approximately 80% of the volume of clays found in Great Britain. This is seen by the following compositions:

PRIMARY CLAY		SECONDARY BALL CLAY		BRICK CLAYS			
SiO_2	46%	SiO_2	60%	SiO_2	60%	CaO	5%
Al_2O_3	40%	Al_2O_3	34%	Al_2O_3	20%	Alkalies	4%
H_2O	14%	Alkalies	2%	Fe_2O_3	8%	Magnesia	3%
		Fe_2O_3 & H_2O	4%				

The same two minerals compose some 50% of the weight of most glazes. They are, therefore, common to both clay and glaze. However, unless a third agent, called a flux or base, is added to the silica and alumina, forming the glaze, it will not melt and adhere to the ceramic during firing. These fluxes have the property of dissolving the silica in the presence of alumina, when heated to certain temperatures, and when mixed in definite proportions. These proportions have been arrived at by much research and experiment, and have proved a sound guide for ceramists.

The bases used in glazes are as follows: lead, soda, potash, calcium and less important bases such as barium, lithium, strontium and magnesium. These are introduced into glaze recipes in their various forms, though mainly as frits or in combination with other elements. Thus, a glaze composed of alumina, silica and a flux or base, when applied and heated, combines with the clay or ceramic article, also composed of alumina, silica and a small proportion of base and other elements.

It is found that most secondary clays contain a small quantity of bases in the form of soda, potash, calcium and magnesia, which, at certain temperatures, melt and cause the body to vitrify and become less porous.

In order to calculate a glaze recipe, it must first be shown as a formula and then converted to the proportions of raw materials that will finally be used. A glaze formula, containing one base such as lead would be shown as follows:

Base		Acid
PbO	$0.3 \, Al_2O_3$	$2.5 \, SiO_2$

The three components react chemically during firing to form a simple or complex aluminium silicate, depending on the amount and type of alkalis present.

Glaze proportions – those of base to acid and acid to alumina – are as follows:

1 unit of base to between 2–4 units of acid, and the proportion of alumina should be between $\frac{1}{5} - \frac{1}{10}$ of the acid.

For hard glazes this is:

1 unit of base to between 3–4 units of acid

and for soft glazes it is:

1 unit of base to between 1·5–3 units of acid, but not less than 1·5 units.

We see from the above formulae, for a soft glaze, using one base, how it applies:

| PbO | $0.3 \, Al_2O_3$ | $2.5 \, SiO_2$ |

Proportion of base to acid is 1 to 2·5, which is between the proportions allowed for soft glazes. The proportion of alumina to acid is ·3 to 2·5, which is between the proportion allowed of $\frac{1}{5} - \frac{1}{10}$ of acid.

In the making of glazes, better results are achieved when more than one base is used. Each base has specific properties, which all add to the qualities of a glaze mix. When more than one base is used, their total still does not exceed 1, for example:

$$\left. \begin{array}{l} 0.5 \, PbO \\ 0.3 \, CaO \\ 0.2 \, K_2O \end{array} \right\} = 1 \text{ unit of base}$$

Because different bases have different properties, and melt at different temperatures, the behaviour of a glaze will depend on the following factors:

1 The number of bases used
2 The type of base or bases used; the number, as well as type of base, affects the fusing point
3 The amount of alumina used
4 The proportion of base to acid, and the presence of boric acid (in addition to silica) which acts as an acid

While there are several bases that can be used in glazes, the main acid, common to them all, is silica.

Because some of the lead compounds begin to volatilize above 1100°C, they are not used in high temperature glazes; here the main bases are calcium, sodium and potassium. Pure oxides of soda, potash and calcium are unstable in their raw state, and combine violently with water. The more stable carbonate of the metal is therefore used in a fritted form, or a ceramic substance containing the base chemically combined, such as soda in felspar.

Before we can prepare a glaze we must be able to translate its formulae (which represents its chemical composition) into a recipe which shows the raw materials to be used, and their quantities. The following list of raw materials, with their chemical composition and molecular weights should be sufficient reference when compiling a wide range of basic glazes:

Raw materials	Chemical formulae	Molecular weight
Litharge	PbO	223
Lead Carbonate	$PbCO_3$	266
Borax (Calcined)	$Na_2B_4O_7$	202
Lead Monosilicate	$PbSiO_3$	283
Lead Bisilicate	$PbO\ 2SiO_2$	343
Lead Sesquisilicate	$PbO\ 1\cdot5SiO_2$	313
Calcium Carbonate	$CaCO_2$	100
China clay or plastic clay	$Al_2O_3\ 2SiO_2\ 2H_2O$	258
Felspar (albite or soda)	$Na_2O\ Al_2O_3\ 6SiO_2$	524
Felspar (potash or orthoclase)	$K_2O\ Al_2O_3\ 6SiO_2$	556
Felspar (Anorthite)	$CaO\ Al_2O_3\ 2SiO_2$	278
Nepheline Syenite (general formula)	$3(Na_2O\ K_2O)\ 4Al_2O_2\ 9SiO_2$	1130–1220
China stone (Purple) (variable)	$\left.\begin{array}{l} 0\cdot012\ MgO \\ 0\cdot157\ CaO \\ 0\cdot340\ K_2O \\ 0\cdot244\ Na_2O \end{array}\right\}\ Al_2O_3\ 6\cdot82SiO_2$	569
China stone (White) (variable)	$\left.\begin{array}{l} 0\cdot048\ MgO \\ 0\cdot204\ CaO \\ 0\cdot280\ K_2O \\ 0\cdot040\ Na_2O \end{array}\right\}\ Al_2O_3\ 7\cdot5SiO_2$	594
Fluorspar	CaF_2	78
Dolomite	$Ca\ Mg\ (CO_3)_2$	184·4
Borocalcite	$CaO\ 2B_2O_3\ 6H_2O$	379
Talc	$3MgO\ 4SiO_2\ H_2O$	304
Flint	SiO_2	60

The molecular weights or unit weights of the raw materials used in glazes are found by adding the atomic weight of each separate element, as shown in all standard lists. For example, Flint – SiO_2: Si = 28, O_2 = 16 × 2 = 32; total 60.

While the proportions already given for compiling glazes are a sound guide, slight adjustments may be necessary once a glaze has been tested. This is because the composition of several of the basic raw materials used may vary with the batch supplied; for example, felspar and china stone tend to be variable.

55

Returning to our original formula, this may now be converted into a glaze recipe as shown by the following chart:

			1 PbO	0·3 Al$_2$O$_3$		2·5 SiO$_2$	
PbO	Al$_2$O$_3$	SiO$_2$	Raw Materials	Molecular Parts	Molecular weight of raw mats.	Parts by weight	Percentage
1	—	—	Litharge	1 ×	222 =	222	54%
	·3	·6	China clay	·3 ×	258 =	77·4	19%
		1·9	Flint	1·9 ×	60 =	114	27%
1	·3	2·5				413·4	100%

In the above chart, the first three columns give the total units of proportion, as shown in the formulae or chemical composition of the glaze. The next column lists the raw materials from which these proportions of alumina, silica and lead are taken. The molecular parts are the proportions or parts of each raw material needed; which, in some cases, will at the same time automatically include a set proportion of other combined elements. These molecular parts, multiplied by the total molecular weight of each raw material, give the parts by weight, which are then converted to a percentage. To explain further, the lead comes from litharge, with no additions. The alumina comes from china clay, which at the same time must give us silica. In china clay we find that for every unit of alumina we must have two units of silica; therefore as we want ·3 of a unit of alumina we must take ·6 of silica which is twice as much by proportion. This leaves us with 1·9 of silica to complete the total; so this is made up with flint, a pure form of silica.

The next formula is for a glaze containing three bases: lead, lime and potash. The lead will come from lead sesquisilicate, a non-poisonous, fritted form of lead, with a high lead content; the lime from whiting; and the soda from felspar:

				Base		Neutral		Acid	
				0·6 PbO					
				0·2 K$_2$O		0·3 Al$_2$O$_3$		2·5 SiO$_2$	
				0·2 CaO					

PbO	K$_2$O	CaO	Al$_2$O$_3$	SiO$_2$	Raw Materials	Molecular Parts	Molecular weight	Parts by weight	Percentage
·6	—	—	—	·9	Lead Sesquisilicate	·6 ×	313 =	187·8	52·6%
	·2	—	·2	1·2	Felspar	·2 ×	556 =	111·2	31·1%
		·2	—	—	Whiting	·2 ×	100 =	20	5·6%
			·1	·2	China clay	·1 ×	25·8 =	25·8	7·2%
				·2	Flint	·2 ×	60 =	12	3·3%
·6	·2	·2	·3	2·5				356·8	99·8%

To simplify this:

The lead comes from lead sesquisilicate, shown on our list with the formula $PbO\ 1\cdot5\ SiO_2$. So for $\cdot6$ of PbO we must have $1\frac{1}{2}$ times as much silica, which is $\cdot9$. The potash comes from the felspar, with the formula $K_2O\ Al_2O_3\ 6\ SiO_2$. Thus to obtain the $\cdot2\ K_2O$ necessary for our glaze, we must accept the proportionate quantities of alumina and silica, which are $\cdot2\ K_2O$, $\cdot2\ Al_2O_3$, $1\cdot2\ SiO_2$.

The calcium comes from whiting, $CaCO_3$ of which we need $\cdot2\ CaO$, the CO_2 being given off as a gas.

At this stage we find that we have our necessary lead, soda and calcium, but are short of alumina by $\cdot1$ of a unit and of silica by $\cdot4$, to make up the necessary total of $\cdot3$ alumina, and $2\cdot5$ silica. The $\cdot1$ of alumina is obtained from china clay with its combined $\cdot2$ of silica. The remaining $\cdot2$ of silica is made up from flint, pure silica.

This glaze, using lead sesquisilicate, is very reliable, not only as a transparent glaze, but for adding colouring oxides and opacifiers. Slight adjustments to the glaze, however, may be necessary according to what oxides, or opacifiers are being added: its firing range is between 1060°C and 1100°C, depending on the clay body and the firing cycle.

Once the broad principle of glaze composition is understood, we should look more closely at the various forms of fluxes, raw materials and colouring oxides in order to discover and assess their particular properties. This will take time, but will be useful for further experiments. Information gleaned in this way should be carefully recorded in a book specially planned, for details concerning glazes. (A list of particularly helpful chemistry books is given in the bibliography.)

Glaze materials

FLUXES The raw forms of lead, such as litharge and lead carbonate, are all suitable for giving great richness to both glazes and colours. They are, however, poisonous, and, if used, must be treated with great care. Their use is only legally permitted in a one-man pottery, or in certain post-graduate art schools.

Unstable bases, such as sodium or potassium, together with raw lead, can be made stable and safe to use by the process of 'fritting'. This, briefly, is carried out by melting the unstable, or poisonous ingredient, with an acid, such as silica, to create a new substance which is ground to a powder and to which only alumina in the correct proportion needs to be added to form a balanced glaze. Frits are cheapest bought ready made.

A very good all round safe frit is lead bisilicate; but because of its high silica content, only a small quantity of additional materials can be added, if the combined lead is the only base. Due to its high silica content, and consequent hardness, glaze containing this fri tends to flake from edges after firing. This may be rectified by a higher firing, or by the addition of another frit containing proportionately less silica.

LEAD SESQUISILICATE, as stated, can be used in many combinations, and in many types of glaze.

CHINA CLAY is a standard source of alumina and silica in the preparation of both stoneware and earthenware glazes. It is also a common matting agent, when some 10%, added to a glaze, is usually sufficient to give a satisfactory result.

CHINA STONE is used mainly in the preparation of stoneware glazes and bodies, and mainly for its alkaline content. However, for earthenware, it contains too high a silica content, which counteracts, too easily, the alkaline content of the china stone at low temperatures.

FELSPAR is used extensively in earthenware glazes to supply the alkaline bases of soda and potash, as well as alumina and silica. It is often the most important constituent of stoneware glazes and in itself contains all the necessary materials for a glaze. While it melts to a white opaque glass at about 1250°C it is not satisfactory used alone.

CALCIUM in the form of whiting is used as a base in both stoneware and earthenware glazes. Used to excess it gives a matt effect, depending upon the temperature.

SILICA in the form of flint or quartz supplies the acid ingredient to all glazes. Another form is silver sand which is almost pure silica.

ZINC OXIDE: ZnO. The properties of this vary greatly, depending on the quantity used in a glaze and the other bases present. Small quantities in excess of 5% can give mattness, due to crystallization on cooling, and a refractory and opaque quality which decreases with an increase in alumina or alkaline base.

Making tests

We will assume that before using a glaze for the first time a small test quantity will be made and fired. This is best carried out on a previously prepared small tile slab, approximately 3×2 in. A supply should always be available, made from the various clays you will be using, and will probably include stoneware as well as earthenware. If you must write the details of your tests in a book, do so, but by far the best method is to write them on the back of the test tile. Paper burns, and books get lost and mislaid, but when the details are fired into the clay, there are no arguments. The tests should then be filed in a flat box for easy reference. Extreme care should be taken when weighing materials for tests, particularly metallic colouring oxides. Here a few grains can greatly affect the intensity of colour. Use the metric system and work with 100 gramme lots of glaze, to which opacifiers or pigments will be added. Unless the additions are to have a very excessive effect on the glaze, they can be calculated as a percentage of the 100 gramme glaze batch. The weights necessary for tests and ceramics generally are as follows:

1	Kilogramme	2	20 gramme	1	500 milligramme or		·5 gramme
2	500 gramme	1	10 ,,	2	200 ,,	,,	·2 ,,
2	150 ,,	2	5 ,,	1	100 ,,	,,	·1 ,,
2	100 ,,	1	2 ,,	2	50 ,,	,,	·05 ,,
1	50 ,,	1	1 ,,	1	25 ,,	,,	·025 ,,

For making tests it is necessary to have a standard set of laboratory scales, though nothing elaborate. These can often be purchased from a second-hand photographic supplier.

For those beginning, the most thorough way to acquire a knowledge of all the raw materials that you intend to use is to make a tabulated test of each raw material on two large white biscuit clay tiles. One can be fired at a standard earthenware temperature and the other at stoneware. This will include your various forms of lead, frits, alkalis, felspars, nepheline syenite, soda ash, whiting, etc. You can then compare the results, showing the same materials fired at these two widely different temperatures.

Assuming that the test proves satisfactory and a large quantity of glaze is then prepared, always test the batch before use. This will save time and cost if a mistake in weighing or calculating has been made. When making the test always apply with two thicknesses, as this can vary the result to a surprising degree, especially with stoneware. As tests fired in a test kiln have a rapid firing cycle, the result should only be taken as an indication, though tests are often surprisingly accurate. If a series of tests is planned, using a particular glaze, mix up a 2,000–3,000 gramme batch, and dry out on a kiln that is firing. From this can be taken 100 gramme lots of dry glaze as required, to which can be added the necessary pigments or opacifiers. Dry glaze is best stored in strong polythene bags, which are available in many sizes. It is easier and quicker to prepare glaze from the dry powder state than from the liquid state, where it may have settled to dense, sticky, rubbery consistency.

Glaze preparation

The choice and preparation of the glaze is very much governed by the type of ceramic to be produced. If your field of activity is wide, it is advisable to stock small quantities of many raw materials (in 2 to 20 lb lots) for carrying out tests and special commissions.

For all work of a general nature it is cheaper and easier to settle for a reliable, all-round glaze, to which can be added pigments, stains, opacifiers or matting agents as required. If you are prepared to order a quantity of at least 1 cwt, most glaze manufacturers will prepare it, using your own formula. It has been proven that it is far more expensive in time and materials to prepare one's own glazes, than to buy them ready made. For those whose ceramics are only a part-time subsidized occupation, the time and cost will matter less.

When glazes are weighed out from dry materials, try to create as little dust as possible, because of the dangers of silicosis from all material containing silica dust. *Never* mix glaze in its dry state, but only after adding water. The degree of grinding and fineness of sieving will depend on the required final result. The finer the grinding and sieving the smoother and more even the fired result, but over-grinding makes glazes crawl. Unground copper, iron, and even cobalt in certain glazes will give a rich textural quality. When a uniformity of finish is required in a coloured glaze, first weigh the pigments and grind them well with sufficient water and a little glaze before adding the main bulk of the batch. When well ground with the pestle and mortar. sieve through a 120-mesh phosphor bronze sieve.

> For sieving glaze use a 120 mesh sieve
> For textured effects use a 80 mesh sieve
> For very fine glazes and some stoneware glazes use a 200 mesh sieve

Always clean these thoroughly before and after use, as a trace of dark pigment remaining from a previous black glaze will contaminate an opaque white glaze which you may be preparing. A useful article for cleaning is a rubber potscraper, or a kidney rubber. The best glaze brushes are known as monkey brushes, and have stiff bristles of suitable length. When possible, all time- and labour-saving devices should be used in a workshop, because the cost of time is by far the most expensive commodity. To assist in the mixing of glazes and slips, a rod with rotor attachment fitted to a portable motor can be invaluable. It is also very useful to have a grindstone attachment to grind off stilt marks after firing. The glaze should be mixed in a polythene bucket or jug, as the rotor will, in time, wear the enamel or metal off any other containers. There is no doubt that many glazes once made improve on standing, but this, of course, is not always possible.

Applying glaze

The thickness of glaze will depend on many factors, and only with continual experience will you become proficient. For example, if the biscuit is very porous, you will need a fairly thin glaze, for if it is applied too thickly it will crack before firing, and this can often be the cause of crawling, as described on page 64.

When the porosity (best tested with the tongue) is almost non-existent, the glaze should be almost as thick as double cream. This also applies to re-glazing over a fired glaze, though if the article is heated first on a kiln that is firing, this is made easier.

Raw glazes being applied to unfired clay need to be thicker than for a biscuited article. This applies as well to many stoneware glazes. Alternatively, a 10% reduced iron stoneware glaze applied thinly, gives a completely different result than when applied thickly: in the first instance a rusty brown, and in the second, a rich black.

For decorative work, the finish of the glaze may be of secondary importance to the colour, but where utility is important this must be given primary consideration, which will generally depend on a high biscuit firing. For earthenware biscuit this can be 1120°C–1180°C.

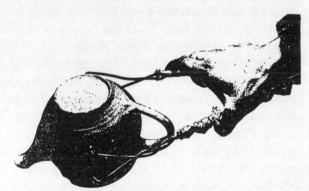

50 Holding a teapot with metal tongs, ready to be glazed by pouring.

Methods of applying glaze

DIPPING   Only suitable when using a large batch of glaze or when glazing a quantity of pieces of much the same size and shape. In this case the best method is to acquire a set of spring steel tongs to grip the articles, and at the same time eliminate the unevenness caused by finger marks. Very large articles can be glazed by holding them with the tongs while the glaze is poured over them from a jug (fig. 50). The most suitable steel for such tongs is a heavy unwound mattress or sofa spring. If, after dipping, the glazed articles are still wet, place them on kiln stilts arranged on boards till the articles are dry enough to handle.

POURING   Perhaps the most difficult technique, if the glaze is not to be splashed in every direction. A large wide bowl is essential and a jugful of glaze which will contain far more

51 Dipping a dish in glaze, using three-pronged tongs. This eliminates all finger marks and the need for touching up before firing.

than you think you will need. Speed and precision are essential and in every case glaze the inside of an article first.

SPRAYING While a small compressor, spray booth, and exhaust fan, are an added cost, I find them invaluable for many glazing jobs. It is not difficult to buy a good second-hand plant that will be adequate for most potters' needs. The disadvantage is the amount of glaze wasted but, as your skill increases, this can be greatly reduced. In time, quantities of waste glaze collect in the spray booth, and can be reused by adding a matting agent and sufficient oxides to make a good matt black glaze. A few glaze firings will soon show up your spraying faults and suggest any changes in technique. When making glaze tests, you can spray small quantities of glaze with little consequent waste. When two or more glazes are to be used on the one area, you can mask and spray with considerable accuracy.

The spray gun should be cleaned immediately after use, as chemicals in the glaze can attack the metals of the gun. Always keep a large bottle of water handy for cleaning out the spray gun and for thinning the glaze if necessary.

Raw glazing

If successful this form of glazing, using only one firing, can reduce costs considerably. Here the glaze must be adjusted by replacing the china clay of the glaze recipe with ball clay, or the clay from which the article is made. This means that the glaze will have a shrinkage equivalent to the raw clay article, and so should not crawl or flake off in drying. So much depends on the physical properties of the clays used; some need to be glazed when very damp and others when bone dry, and I have often glazed raw clay with a standard biscuitware glaze with excellent results. It is therefore not possible to lay down hard and fast rules in this matter; one must rely upon practical experience.

An approach to using glazes

There has never been any disagreement concerning the undeniable qualities of a well-fired stoneware body and glaze, but how often one sees stoneware articles where the only quality is that obtained by the high reduction firing. Alas, for earthenware this does not follow. Apart from certain rich, bright coloured glazes, the result depends far more on painstaking experiment and control where the result must be known and calculated. So

61

much will depend on the exact composition of the glaze, the speed of firing and accurate temperature control. It is only natural, therefore, that beginners usually prefer to work in stoneware because it appears less difficult and the problems of decoration are less pressing. Earthenware must either be well decorated or enhanced with an attractive glaze; by its very nature some form of adornment is necessary. Once the time and effort involved in the preliminary work on earthenware glazes has been carried out, the range of possibilities for colour, texture, and treatment will be considerable. This will then be invaluable for those who wish to tackle the many challenges facing the ceramist in this field today.

While we see around us so much earthenware ruined by bad decoration and lack of colour sense, there is still a very large market for good ceramics where colour and decoration are predominant. So often I am asked why so much hand-made pottery must be dull in colour. The answer is not difficult to find. It obviously entails much hard work and imagination and this challenge has been largely evaded and ignored in Britain.

The firing of glazes and bodies is very similar to cooking, where exact control of heat and firing time are absolutely necessary. Thickness of ware and glaze must be related to time and temperature. For the individual ceramist, control of firing and consequent adequate maturing of glaze and body are essential to quality, especially in earthenware work.

Glaze tests in earthenware

To begin glaze tests we could return to our standard lead, lime and potash glaze, and carry out a series of experiments where the whole range of possible proportions, between the silica and the base, are worked out. This could then be repeated and, in each instance, a set percentage of a colouring oxide (e.g., 6% of iron oxide) could be added to the glaze to observe its effect. Following this, glazes should be compiled using widely varying bases from pure lead, to leadless and alkaline, such as:

a) A raw litharge lead base only; b) a glaze with three bases, containing a fritted lead, together with lime and potash; c) an alkali-based glaze.

When fired, compare their quality and note the visual and tactile differences.

Next, make a series of tests, adding to the above different opacifiers: tin, zircon, zinc, etc., using approximately 10%. Then test the reaction of different basic metallic pigments such as copper, iron, etc., both on and under these glazes. Do this in both the opaque and the transparent state, applying the pigments with a brush in varying degrees of intensity.

Next, take a well-balanced glaze, such as the lead, lime and potash glaze, using the lead sesquisilicate already mentioned, and prepare a large quantity. Take 100 gramme or 50 gramme dry lots, and combine them in turn with a graded quantity of each of the metal oxides, using copper, cobalt manganese, iron, chrome, nickel and antimoniate of lead, and tin. This will give an accurate indication of the varying degrees of intensity of the different pigments when added in increasing quantities; e.g., *basic glaze* plus ·5% copper oxide, 1%, 2%, 4%, 6%, 8% and 10%, and the same for the rest of the colouring pigments.

Now take one of these series of coloured glazes, this time adding a set percentage of opacifier, say 8%. Again, take the same series, and add a set percentage of another colouring oxide. For example, ·5% of copper oxide with 1%, 2%, 4%, 6%, 8% and 10% of yellow glaze stain or antimoniate of lead, and compare these with the tests using the yellow only.

This is just a beginning but will suggest endless possibilities. The importance of this exercise, is to learn how to match and relate colours, which is invaluable when ceramics are being used in an interior to form part of an overall colour scheme.

With the same basic glaze, make a series of tests for black glazes where one of the three oxides predominate to give either a warm, cold, blue-black, or metallic quality and all are fired at the same temperature of 1060°C.

(a)		(b)		(c)		(d)	
7%	Ferric	6%	CoO	2%	Ferric	7%	Mn
2%	Mn	2%	Mn.	3%	CuO	3%	CoO
1%	Cobalt	1%	CuO	3%	Mn		

This may then be varied according to needs, and if too soft for the temperature, counteract with an addition of china clay.

Returning to the basic glaze, make further tests with increasing quantities of china clay or whiting to observe the increasing degree of mattness and behaviour of the glaze. If calcined alumina is used alone less will be needed, as a very small quantity is required to give a matt surface. From this can follow matt coloured glazes. However, these are difficult to control in firing when used on large articles or pots.

Besides a lead-based glaze, tests should be carried out with both colours and matting agents added to an alkaline glaze that has proved suitable in earlier experiments. In making tests for turquoise-blue using an alkaline base, it must be remembered that the addition of alumina will cause the copper to remain green.

Stoneware

A comparatively unexplored field of experiment for studio potters is the use of more colour in oxidized stoneware. Artigas gives many ideas in his book of glazes (see Bibliography). The use of cobalt and iron, manganese, rutile, copper and other combined oxides, would yield fruitful results. While qualities of glaze remain constant fashions and tastes will change, so the ceramist should be able to vary his field or he may find he is producing for a non-existent market.

Porcelain

Porcelain glazes have a distinctive quality and here colour used with imagination and discretion can achieve a quality unobtainable in any other medium.

Frits

Fritting is the melting of two or more glaze constituents to form a new substance which is cooled, broken up and ground to a powdered state. Before being fritted, some of these materials are soluble in water and therefore unsatisfactory for use in glazes; other materials, such as raw lead, are poisonous and made safe for use by fritting.

Frits used in glazes tend to settle out quickly and need constant stirring. This is due to their lack of plasticity and, by adding 1 to 2% of bentonite or certain other jelling agents, the fritted materials will remain longer in suspension.

Glaze faults

CRAZING Because the composition and properties of a body and the applied glaze are different and variable, it is understandable that they will tend to behave in different ways when heated, or on cooling. Therefore, if the shrinkage of a glaze on cooling is greater than the body, the resulting tensions will cause the glaze to crack or craze. The greater the strain, the more the crazing. When the glaze, however, is under slight compression, the tendency to craze is eliminated. This, of course, is governed by the co-efficient of expansion which, in this case, will be lower for the glaze than for the body. If, however, the compression is too great, we get the opposite of crazing, which is peeling or flaking. Here the glaze tends to scale from edges and, in extreme cases, will shatter the body or split it when cooling. Peeling may also be caused by soluble salts which have collected, particularly on the edges of the ware, during drying, and then during firing have prevented the glaze from firmly combining with the body.

In order to overcome crazing caused by the varying co-efficient of expansion of body and glaze, the following general rules can be of assistance:

(i) *When the body is constant* Increase the amount of silica in the glaze, or substitute some of the silica with boric acid. As highly alkaline glazes craze more than lead- or barium-based glazes, replace the potash or soda base with lead or barium. The addition of a little china clay or alumina to a glaze can often abolish crazing. Another cure can be to fire the glaze for a longer, or alternatively higher period.

(ii) *When the glaze is constant* One of the first things to do is to fire the biscuit to a higher temperature or to fire it for a longer period. As well-calcined flint is more effective than sand or quartz in eliminating crazing, reduce the clay content of the body and increase the flint. An added help is to use finer ground flint or quartz, but if it becomes too fine the ware will tend to dunt on cooling. Another method is to reduce the fluxes and alumina in a body; this is best done by reducing the felspar which contains alkaline (fluxes) and alumina.

For all cases of peeling, carry out the opposite remedies to those for crazing.

CRAWLING This is caused by often invisible cracks in the glaze surface after application, particularly when the glaze is thick and contains a lot of china clay, considerable shrinkage occurring. This can be overcome by gently rubbing the glaze when dry, in order to eliminate the cracks. In shrinking, the glaze tends to lift, and this obviously is difficult to detect. On fusing and melting, the glaze, then, does not settle and adhere to the biscuit, but draws away and forms what we term crawling. Crawling can also occur if the biscuit is slightly dusty, greasy or vitreous when glazed. This then acts as a deterrent to the melting glaze, causing it to crawl. Another cause can be too-softly-fired biscuit which continues to shrink in the glaze firing, giving uneven tensions with the glaze. Others can be over-grinding of the glaze or colours, or too much magnesia in a glaze.

BUBBLING This can be caused by under-firing (a dry surface), or over-firing when the glaze literally boils. These bubbles are very sharp and the glaze surface extremely shiny.

Fine bubbles in a glaze are caused by gases given off in the firing which do not escape, and can remain when the glaze is later fired to an even higher temperature. It is also noticeable when certain transparent glazes are too thickly applied.

64

8 · Kilns and firing

Different branches of the ceramic industry tend to use specific forms of fuel for firing. However, where in the past the bulk of them relied on solid fuel with its consequent high percentage of waste, most today rely on gas, electricity and, to an increasing extent, oil fuel. Obviously electricity is the cleanest, and in many ways the most efficient. Cost of fuel is, of necessity, a determining factor when deciding on the type of kiln to instal.

For the types of ceramic we discuss, the main sources of heat are electricity and gas, with oil fuel on the increase.

Electricity

In an electric kiln the elements are not unlike those of an electric heater; they are set in the walls of the kiln and radiate the heat, which is thermostatically controlled. Its advantages are reasonable cost and control, together with greater safety and cleanliness in firing.

For stoneware firing electricity is only suitable when oxidizing, but for regular firings at temperatures above 1280°C the element loss can be considerable.

In practically all modern electric kilns the elements are exposed and so arranged that considerable evenness of temperature can be achieved in the final stages of firing. The life of a kiln depends very much upon the way it has been used, how regularly it has been fired, and the pattern of firing cycles. A kiln fired regularly twice a week all the year round, can last for at least ten to fifteen years and sometimes even longer, with, of course, the periodic replacement of elements. It is always cheaper to renew worn elements before they actually burn out and cause great inconvenience. If treated with care it is surprising how long elements will last. The golden rule is to disturb them as little as possible. In time they acquire a protective oxidized coating which, if disturbed, shortens their life and weakens the elements where the coating is fractured. While it hurts any ceramist to fire a kiln when empty, to do so occasionally is good for the elements. The elements are attacked by certain gases given off during firing, and the effect of firing in a purely oxidizing atmosphere cleans the coating and prolongs their life. In time they turn dark brown in colour, and small areas of darker eruptions, or patches, become visible on the coils; immediately this happens they should be replaced.

When firing electric kilns, it is very important to have adequate ventilation, not only in the early stages when moisture and gases are given off, but throughout the firing. Lack of ventilation can soon create a reducing atmosphere which can have an adverse effect on bodies, glazes, and the elements. Some kilns have ventilation holes in the back wall.

For beginners, a very good small and relatively inexpensive kiln is one with an approximate internal dimension of 15 × 15 × 16 in. For a little extra it can be fitted with high temperature elements suitable for a stoneware firing, if required. Medium sized kilns, 18 × 18 × 24 in internal dimensions, and larger ones are also available.

Before buying any electric kiln, check how near you are to mains electricity. If you plan to place your kiln some distance from the mains it may cost more than the kiln itself to have the power extended. More costly still is the installation of wiring to take your kiln load, if heavier than the existing supply.

Gas

Gas is normally used more for industrial than individual ceramics; it is, however, a very good form of fuel for studio potters, because of the wide range of firing techniques that it will cover. The main difficulty is the need (particularly in built-up and urban areas) for adequate flue ventilation. In some areas by-laws can be very tricky. Its advantages are a wide firing range, from earthenware through to porcelain, and from an oxidizing atmosphere to a reducing one, so necessary for producing celadons and iron rust glazes in stoneware.

With gas the most suitable form of kiln is a full sealed muffle, where the flames are excluded, but which surround and heat the firing chamber or muffle. Gas kilns are generally more expensive than electric kilns.

Oil firing

With oil firing, the cheapness of fuel can be an attractive factor in some countries. However, this can often vary alarmingly by the sudden imposition of taxes, particularly where oil for heating is not widely used. For stoneware firings requiring both oxidation and reduction, it is an excellent fuel, but less satisfactory for earthenware, unless the ware is well protected from the direct flame. Oil gives a fierce concentrated heat, and only at high temperatures does it have a more even distribution. In the early stages of firing the heat is naturally concentrated near the burners, where high resistant refractories are needed in a kiln's construction.

Fuel with clay

A further word might be said here regarding fuel added to clay. This method of assisting firing is often practised in more primitive societies. Even today it is used in the brick industry, where it can be efficiently controlled.

In the case of bricks, the fuel used is a form of coke dust, but in peasant societies the use of dung, wood-pulp, and often the spongy tops of bulrushes are used. If these mixtures are fired in an oxygen-starved atmosphere (not unusual in primitive firings) rich black to brown coloured bodies result, particularly if they already contain a high iron content.

Wood firing

Where wood is plentiful and inexpensive this can be a very good form of fuel, giving high temperatures and comparatively clean firings. For earthenware firings it is more satisfactory to place the ware in protecting saggars, but for stoneware oxidisation or reduction, open firing is generally practised. Constant attention and care in stoking is essential throughout the firing, making it a long arduous task, which may take up to thirty-six hours or more.

Coal firing

Coal is still used in many places throughout the world, but seldom in the firing of small kilns. Here the cleaner-firing coke is more common.

Drying clay wares before firing

This is an extremely important stage in all ceramic production. Drying should never be hurried or forced, unless this can be done with gentle even heat to all surfaces of the article. For instance, if it is not possible to keep turning large ceramic slabs, because of relief modelling etc., they should be allowed to dry slowly, protected from direct draughts, or direct sunlight. If large flat slabs of clay are dried too rapidly they will lift at the corners. When this happens they will remain in this distorted state, should they be fired even to stoneware temperatures. Thrown articles may be placed in the sun for drying as soon as they are made, but their position should be altered regularly. Depending of course upon the latitude, the season, and the size of the thrown shape, pots left in the sun may be ready for turning or for the application of handles within an hour.

When possible, avoid any unnecessary weight or strain on the rims of wide shallow containers and dishes, as this may cause cracking. The coarser the clay mixture, the greater the care necessary in handling the dry unfired article; and alternatively, the more plastic the clay, the tougher it is. Faults, and damage to ware by careless handling are often only apparent after the biscuit firing. Unfortunately, by this time the bulk of an article's cost has been incurred.

Firings

Once a clay article has been thoroughly air-dried it is fired to the required biscuit temperature. When cool it is safe for handling and may be glazed or decorated, according to the required result; it is then glaze fired. It is possible to combine these operations in one firing, but it needs great care and skill in both handling and firing.

Firing ranges

As a general rule the following ranges are a good guide.

EARTHENWARE 1000°C to 1180°C   Most white or buff earthenware biscuit is best fired to 1080°C or above, though the industry normally fires from 1120°C to 1180°C. For glaze firing the temperature is generally between 1060°C and 1100°C, although for some glazes a higher or lower temperature is preferable.

STONEWARE 1200°C to 1300°C   For stoneware the biscuit firing can be done at earthenware temperatures. Most stoneware glazes mature between 1250°C and 1300°C. Biscuit and glaze firings may be combined in one firing, though sometimes stoneware is left unglazed because when fired it is vitreous and non-porous.

PORCELAIN 1280°C to 1400°C   Here again the biscuit fire can be comparatively soft, or with careful raw glazing, in some instances, it can be dispensed with.

Reducing

The principle of reduction is to restrict or reduce the supply of air entering the kiln in order to create an atmosphere where complete combustion cannot take place, due to the absence of sufficient oxygen.

This process begins at about 1100°C when the oxygen atoms in the glaze and body are said to become unstable and more active. While the air is restricted the fuel is not, so that much of it changes to free carbon or smoke. The hot carbon avidly combines with the oxygen atoms in the body and glaze in order to complete its combustion. This naturally changes the composition (and consequently the colour) of the iron-oxide in both glaze and body by reducing it to a lower oxide. Hence ferric oxide, Fe_2O_3, is reduced to ferrous oxide, FeO. Slight continuous, or regular heavy reduction, is then induced till the end of the firing.

In an open kiln the firing fuel acts as the reducer. However, if a muffle kiln is used, the fuel is inserted through a spy-hole in the form of a gas jet or solid fuel that readily gives off free carbon.

Pale blue to green celadons are obtained by adding approximately $2\frac{1}{2}\%$ iron oxide to the glaze. Rust red is possible when a glaze containing 10% of iron oxide is added and applied thinly. The same glaze applied thickly gives a very rich black.

While reducing, great care should be taken in arranging adequate ventilation for any excess unfired gases formed, such as carbon monoxide, that may have escaped from the kiln. If reducing with a gas jet, first check to make sure that the composition of the gas is suitable for giving a reducing atmosphere. (There are also very real dangers, when lighting a gas kiln, if too much gas escapes before ignition takes place). If excessive reduction takes place before the required temperature is reached, the free carbon in the muffle will enter the unfused glaze, and no amount of firing or heat will remove it. When the kiln is unpacked, there will be dark areas of grey to black on the sides of the ware; this is more likely to occur in the cooler areas of the kiln. When reducing with solid fuel make sure that the wares adjacent to the fuel entry are protected from the direct action of its spontaneous ignition.

Biscuit firing

This is the most important stage for many clays, but one that is not always given the necessary care. In clay two forms of water are present, water of formation and chemically combined water. The water of formation is forced from the clay by air drying, or heating, in a suitable atmosphere of up to about 150°C; while chemically combined water is expelled from the clay only by heating in a kiln, which takes place between 450°C and 600°C when the kiln begins to show dull red. Before this, at 200°C, the organic matter in the clay begins to decompose and fire away.

At the critical stage of 450–600°C the temperature increase must be extremely gradual and slow. This is to allow the chemically combined moisture to escape, which it does in the form of steam given off in considerable volume. The thicker the clay, the further and slower must the steam travel. If the temperature is raised too rapidly, sudden steam pressure builds up, and the sudden expansion consequently shatters the ware. While the steam is escaping, plenty of ventilation in the kiln is required to draw off the volumes of steam. When the chemically combined water has been driven from the clay a chemical change takes place, and the clay can never regain its plastic state.

From some 350°C upwards a process of oxidization occurs when the organic matters ignite, together with sulphur compounds and carbon, which do not completely fire away till about 900°C. Above 600°C the temperature can be increased steadily till the fusing or vitrifying state is approached. This will vary with the type of clay. A slower firing, at this stage, allows the heat time to penetrate the ware evenly, and commence the process of vitrification.

At this temperature the softest fluxes in the clay begin to melt, and it is then that the firing is terminated, before the clay has completely fused, leaving no porosity. This is sometimes referred to as arrested reaction, the complete reaction being the fusing and then melting of the clay.

If the biscuit firing should continue at this point, the fluxes in the body would begin to dissolve the silica and other materials, fuse together and render the clay non-porous. With a continuing increase of heat, the clay would become softer and melt to a glass, and form a frothy matrix on the floor of the kiln. In practice, however, the firing range from vitrifying to melting, can be very wide and gradual, being greatly affected by the clay's composition.

For fine earthenware, vitrification occurs between 1100–1200°C.

For terracotta wares, bricks and red tiles, 900–1040°C.

For most studio earthenwares, 1040–1140°C.

For stoneware, 1200–1280°C.

Porcelain is different, in that it changes its substance at temperatures above 1300°C, when alumina and silica combine to form a crystalline material called mullite. While in an earthenware biscuit firing, the clay will have shrunk some 8% or $\frac{1}{12}$, there is a period, up to 800°C when the clay actually expands, before continuing to contract. I have seen a large bottle kiln full of stacked flowerpots, bread bins and jugs expand during firing and forced against the dome of the kiln, chipping pieces off the top layer of pots. Fired biscuit should cool as slowly as possible, particularly in the lower temperature ranges. In conclusion, we can say that for all forms of biscuit firing, the temperature rise should be slow and steady till the chemically combined water is driven off; then the temperature may be increased more rapidly, till nearing vitrification point, when 'soaking' is necessary to even out the temperature in the kiln, and allow the heat to penetrate evenly the thicker ware.

The simplest test for porosity is to see how quickly moisture applied with the tongue is absorbed into the biscuit. Another method is to tap the edge of the article with a hard object, and note the quality of ring. This will be sharp and clear if well fired, but a dull flat note if the biscuit ware is softly fired.

Glaze firing for earthenware

In glaze firing it is the later stages that are the most critical. The firing can begin and continue fairly rapidly until the glaze begins to melt. From here until the end of the firing, the increase in temperature should be very gradual, in order to permit the necessary chemical reactions to take place in the glaze, and at the same time allow the glaze to adhere to the surface of the article. There is a minimum period necessary for allowing a glaze to fully mature, and this should not be hurried or shortened. The average time for a glaze firing is some nine to eleven hours.

For earthenware, the application of glaze is mainly to counter porosity by sealing the surface of the ware, and at the same time give it a hard wearing surface. It therefore follows that, if the biscuit firing has been adequate, then differences in glaze temperatures are possible. For more ornamental wares, the finished colour and decorations of the ceramic can be more important than an attempted impervious surface.

Glaze firing for stoneware

Here the pattern of firing is similar to that of earthenware. The main difference is in the fact that when the glaze has matured, the body should be completely vitrified and non-porous. In a stoneware firing, the fusion of glaze and body is more intense. Because of the higher temperatures, a stoneware firing takes longer than an earthenware. Depending upon the size of the kiln, it may take from twelve to eighteen hours.

Packing an earthenware biscuit kiln

While some people fire biscuit lower than glaze, this is unadvisable, unless there are no alternatives; for if the highest temperature is that for biscuit, the defects likely to occur will be apparent after this first firing. The maximum shrinkage will have taken place, and any distortions will have occurred, as well as changes in colour.

There is no difficulty in packing single free standing articles where no stress or damage from other wares is likely to occur. Great care should be exercised when packing ware in stacks. The weight should be evenly distributed, by arranging the points of contact as far as possible in alignment. When stacking bowls or dishes it is a help to place them in a shape that has already been biscuit fired and filled with sand, in such a way as to support the shape of the unfired wares. At the same time a little silver sand is placed between the pieces in the stack, to prevent the biscuit ware sticking, to distribute the weight evenly, and to absorb any pigment that may volatilize or flash during the firing. This occurs when dishes have been decorated with pigment in the raw clay state, and if this precaution is not taken, the pattern will be transferred to the back of the dish immediately above, and stain the glaze when fired.

Most thick flat pieces of ceramic should be gently worked into a thin bed of sand, when packing, for overall support and to allow easy movement when shrinkage takes place during firing. It is equally important that large slabs be placed away from the elements which, in an electric kiln, give localized heat in the early stages of firing. Uneven heat causes tensions within the clay, which may produce cracking. This also applies when the same articles are fired in a glaze kiln, where the heat increase should also be very gradual to begin with.

Tall thin articles placed too near the source of heat often contract unevenly, the result being some lopsided pots. It is costly to reverse and refire, in the hope of straightening them.

Packing an earthenware glaze kiln

While there are sound reasons for firing biscuit and glaze separately, circumstances may sometimes prevent it. In this case, the ware should be divided and placed at different levels in the kiln, to ensure that the volatilizing glaze does not mark any biscuit placed near it. Kiln shelves used for glaze firings should be brushed with a coating of water and flint before use to facilitate cleaning, should any glaze become attached to the shelves during firing. An even better, and inexpensive, wash is that containing equal parts of zircon and china clay, with water. Less damage will be done to a shelf treated in this way, should the glazed base of a pot be placed by mistake directly on it.

52 Single 'bits', shallow and tall stilts, and an egg stilt. These are the minimum requirements for supporting glazed ware in the kiln.

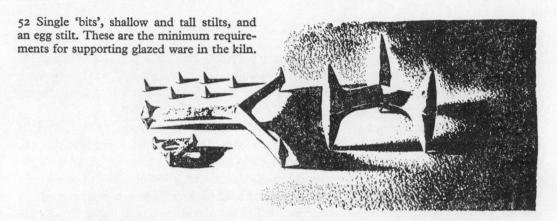

Where practical, articles should have a footring, which can be cleaned, for easy placing when glaze firing. When this is not possible the article should be well supported by some form of stilt. One of the most suitable is 'bits' (fig. 52). These can be placed singly where ever desired, and, being small, use up a minimum of height in a kiln. Three-pronged stilts of various sizes are suitable for most wares. When tiles are being fired in any quantity, columns of stacking tile shelves for placing, are the most efficient and economical.

As with biscuit, do not place glazed articles too near the elements in an electric kiln, or the surface of ware adjacent to the elements will over-fire and the glaze may bubble.

Packing for a stoneware glaze firing

For stoneware the shelves must be treated with flint or a thin layer of sand and the articles always fired firmly on their base. This is important, because the fused stoneware body can often adhere to the kiln shelf, chipping the base of the articles or causing them to fracture during cooling. Stoneware pots should never be stilted, as the support of the whole base is necessary at these high temperatures. It is also advisable, when glazing, to clean the glaze well away from the footring, and at the same time not to glaze the base.

Cooling

As a general rule stoneware should be allowed to cool as slowly as possible, because rapid cooling, particularly at low temperatures, can crack and fracture the ware.

9 · Equipment and management of a small pottery

Kilns and wheels

The first and most necessary piece of equipment is a kiln. This need not exceed one cubic foot in capacity. I know many students who have started work in this way, producing work in their vacations and, when the need arose, buying larger kilns. Most kiln manufacturers offer very favourable credit terms.

While there are some ceramists who seldom use a wheel, there are others for whom it is indispensable. Many types of potters' wheels have been used since pots were first thrown, and though a great deal may depend on one's early tuition, our choice of wheel today is very much a personal matter. Some people are convinced that good pots can be made only on a kick wheel. If jigger and jolly work is contemplated, this is best carried out on an industrial-type wheel, but, unless its speed is adjusted, it will be less suitable for studio-throwing; however, these wheels last longer, but cost much more.

Materials

So much will depend on the space available for storage and working, when ordering clay, raw materials and equipment.

Briefly, the minimum equipment and materials would include the following:

Kiln and shelves, plus spares to cover breakages, with two or three spare elements in case of failure.

Kiln shelf props, plus a few extras.

Seger temperature cones, if no pyrometer is used. You will need these in any case should the pyrometer break down.

Two gross each of a limited range of stilts, 'bits' included. 'Arrowsmiths' have an excellent catalogue.

One hundredweight of silver sand for use in biscuit firings and general production.

Clay supplied wrapped in polythene sheets. Check at least a one hundredweight lot on arrival, to make sure it is the correct clay, and, more important still, is clean. If not, let the supplier know and return it immediately. If this is delayed, they will seldom take responsibility.

Two tubs or bins for soaking clay.

Nylon wire for cutting clay, and trimming clay in dishes.

A large lidded drum or bin for preparing and storing casting slip if used.

Two hundredweight of potters' plaster, for moulds, plaster throwing bats (made on a 12 in wheelhead), and slabs for clay drying.

A rubber kidney to completely clean the container after having mixed plaster. Drains get blocked very easily and plumbers are gold-plated.

A wide strip of lino, or thin sheet brass for cottling moulds, and a supply of rubber rings cut from a car or lorry inner tube, are invaluable.

Soft soap, that should be diluted by heating two parts of soap to one of water, and then bottling until ready for use.

A banding wheel for decorating and mould making. This is also necessary for glaze spraying.

Raw materials for glazes (Minimum)

28 lb   felspar, flint, chinastone, china clay, ball clay, whiting and quartz, lead sesqui-silicate, lead bi-silicate, and an alkaline frit.

3–5 lb   copper oxide, cobalt oxide, manganese oxide, antimoniate of lead or yellow glaze stains, tin oxide.

8–10 lb   iron oxide.

Any other glaze stains or colours.

1 lb soda ash and sodium silicate for making casting slip.

Workshop tools

Turning tools. Metal strips, flexible steel palettes, file, carborundum, or grindstone. Modelling tools. Metal modelling tools for moulds and general work. An indelible pencil. Packing case metal strip for turning tools. Surform blade for trimming the edges of dishes and many clay wares. Two to three good natural sponges for fettling. One large synthetic sponge for cleaning up. Slip trailer with nozzles. A large wooden cylinder for rolling clay. A piece of coarse but close-weave sacking, on which to roll clay.

Selection of good but cheap brushes for pigments, wax, etc. Two or three quality brushes for special work. Wax and paraffin. A large set-square for cutting slabs or tiles. A 3 ft × 2 in × $\frac{1}{8}$ in steel bar for cutting straight edges to flat pieces of clay; wood warps too quickly.

A large pestel and mortar for grinding glazes. A small pestel and mortar for tests and pigments. Two 120-mesh phosphor bronze sieves. Two 80-mesh ditto. Three sieve brushes. A set of polythene bowls and jugs if possible. A prepared bottle of gum for adding to glaze when required. Polythene bags for storing glaze when dry. Spring steel tongs for glazing.

General materials

Polyfilla and white cement for pointing or 'grouting'. Damp cupboard or box for keeping articles moist. Boards of standard size for carrying, placing and storing ware.

Adhesives

FOR SLABS AND TILES When not using cement and sand, or metal clamps, rubber-based adhesives are the most satisfactory for heavy external units.

FOR JOINING AND STICKING to metal, wood, marble, glass, etc:

For indoor use, rubber-based or water-bound adhesives can be used. The toughest for joining are the resin-based plastics containing a filler to which a small quantity of catalyst is added.

Precautions

It is as well to remember here that your most precious instruments are your hands which can easily become damaged if used too violently for beating clay. The nerves in the palms, if damaged, can make potting almost impossible and have been the cause of many people having to severely restrict their work.

Find out from a doctor or weight-lifter the correct methods for lifting and carrying weights. This is extremely important when loading heavy kiln shelves.

We all know the danger from lead poisoning, but how many of us are aware of the poisonous qualities of copper carbonate, barium compounds and antimony, both singly and as antimoniate of lead.

Business and costing

As soon as you sell your first piece of work you are in business. You may not realize it for some time, but there are methods and patterns of business and economics that will, in time, be unavoidable. Some people believe in learning the hard way, but, for instance, the path could be made easier by reading *The Law and the Profits*, by Professor C. Northcote Parkinson, in which he serves cold facts with a delicious spice of humour. He has also written other books on the subject.

When you begin, no matter in how modest a way, record every money transaction; and even before you begin seek the advice of an accountant. They know their job and expect you to know yours. Do not leave accounts for a year or more, thinking that your small turnover is too insignificant to be worthy of attention. It may then take several years to sort out your papers – if you can find them, and convince the Inland Revenue that you do hope one day to make a profit, and are not just a tax dodger. The tax men are both human and experienced at the game.

COSTING   This is a very important part of every business, and in broad principle is as follows:

Fixed Costs (incurred annually):
Rent or mortgage. Rates and insurance. Heating and Lighting. Telephone. Fuel, firing, etc. Accountants' fees. Wages, if staff are employed. Cleaning, and laundry.

Extras (but not necessarily yearly):
Equipment, from kilns and office needs, to buckets and sponges. Attorney's or solicitor's fees (for lease, etc.). Cost of packaging, etc., used in the course of a year. Repairs (various), plumbing, wiring, etc. Redecorating of premises. Catalogue and price list.

You will soon be able to estimate your approximate yearly outlay, which can then be reduced to a monthly or weekly expenditure. To these overheads must be added the cost of the raw materials, before any ceramics are made.

The time it takes you for making, which can represent your wages, may possibly be added earlier, on a weekly basis, because there will be much of the week when you are carrying out work that is called non-productive. This will include writing letters, visiting clients or customers, talking to visitors, etc., and all this time has to be paid for. Make a regular addition when costing, for depreciation, so that when the time comes, in theory at least, you should have the money to buy that new kiln. Only when all this has been calculated and related proportionately to any or each article, can you decide whether you can sell it at an economic price when you have added a certain percentage as profit.

Another quick method of costing is to calculate the exact quantity of biscuit and glazed ware your kiln or kilns can fire in one week. You must now balance the total cost of time, materials, overheads and planned profit margin, against the value of ware that must be realised by every kiln firing. This holds good for production ceramics which are uniform in type. You will naturally take into consideration your kiln capacity and the potential value of its contents when giving an estimate for a large project. Your overheads remain constant, whereas your working costs will fluctuate.

It is fatal to base costs on bargain conditions that one may be temporarily enjoying, such as low rent, etc. Therefore assess your rent for overheads, as being near an open market value for an equivalent property; so that, should you be forced suddenly to find new premises, you will more easily afford them. Many potters fail to cost their own time at a sufficiently high rate, so that when additions to the family arrive there is nothing over to support them.

Make allowances for unforseen costs. When a buyer tells you there is a good market for certain articles, because they are scarce, be cautious – you will almost invariably find on checking that others, and now you, can just not afford to make them. A small article takes as much, or more time to make than a large one – though it usually takes longer to sell the large one. Always remember the old saying 'Better an idle fool than a busy one'.

Some craftsmen attend classes, or take short courses in general business practice and costing. This will obviously pay dividends. In America, many ceramic students automatically complete their training with a course in business methods.

Transacting business

A degree of enthusiasm is essential, but be careful to avoid creating a demand that you are not prepared either to fulfil, or to continue supplying. As a rule, apart from your own individual work, do not make a practice of carrying out work unless it is definitely ordered or is selling well. Do not work on a sale or return basis, except on rare occasions and under special conditions, such as for exhibitions.

The buyer for a store is conditioned to expect delays, excuses, unreliability and mistakes; so if you plan to be in business for some time, the best course is to try to prove him wrong, and to show him that the pass-word for all potters is not 'mañana, mañana'! It pays.

If you send statements regularly at the end of every month, people will see that you mean business. However, if you are irregular with your bills, the customer soon becomes irregular with payments. Accounts should always be monthly, and if your customer continues to owe money after three months, seek your accountant's advice. Keep a carbon copy of every letter you write, even in longhand.

Selling

'How', it is often said, 'do I set about selling?' You soon find that while you are selling, or finding a market, you are not producing. When you are busy producing, well, nothing gets sold. This, of course, becomes less of a dilemma, once your markets have been established.

Outlets for individual products include exhibitions, special displays, and personal recommendation. Features and editorial mention in magazines may also greatly assist in the sales of this type of work.

There are two courses open to the potter for the direct selling of standard wares. One is to employ an agent. The other is to stop production for a period, and to visit as many shops as possible taking orders, and returning afterwards to execute them. These visits may be made twice a year – starting in January for the summer market, and July or August for the Christmas market.

If you decide to employ an agent, remember that he works on a commission basis. This is generally in the region of ten to fifteen per cent of the wholesale price, which must be allowed for in your costing. The more he sells for you, the richer he becomes, and the more work you have to produce. You then soon find the limit to what one pair of hands can achieve in a given time – obviously not enough to keep you and the agent alive. Most agents represent many firms and products, so he may be content with your small contribution.

Dealing with clients

This is on a more personal level, where a great deal of time may be spent before a project even commences. Larger sums of money are usually involved, so the client may be slow to make decisions. It is easy, but unwise, to become too involved with work before a commission is officially confirmed. An honest client will often agree to pay any initial costs, if a project does not materialize. When costing and working on special projects, one often finds that the initial cost involved in discussions, designing and trials, can sometimes account for as much as fifty per cent of the total estimate.

Once a project is confirmed, make sure that any additional work, or cost, is mutually agreed. It is always wise after a meeting, to write immediately and confirm what you have just discussed. If you receive no reply, it is legally assumed that the client is in agreement.

When someone wishes to commission work, for which they say there is only a limited budget, don't fall for the prestige carrot! 'You know, old man, if you like to do this at the price, you will get a great deal of publicity. Our clients are big people, you know – could put a lot of work in your way.' Obviously the better you are known, the more work you may sell; but only lend pieces when you have them to spare. If any are broken or stolen while on loan there is every chance that you will get their value in insurance, so check that the borrower is well covered.

Take advice, and legal advice at that, before beginning a partnership. For every one that succeeds, nine fail.

Glossary

BLUNGER Container with paddle rotor arm for mixing slips.

CASTING SLIP Liquid clay with a low water content where the fluidity has been induced by the addition of chemicals called deflocculents.

DEFLOCCULENT A chemical added to clay which disperses the particles and, with the addition also of a little water, causes fluidity.

DEVITRIFY To crystallize out on cooling. This is common when using unfritted alkaline bases in a glaze.

DUNTING The cracking of ware while cooling due to stresses or too rapid cooling.

FRIT To fuse by heating the poisonous or water soluble bases with a proportion of silica to make them safer or non-soluble. When cool the 'frits' are ground to a powder for use in glazes.

FETTLING The trimming and cleaning of the edges and seams of cast articles, and of all forms of clayware.

FIRE CLAY A plastic refractory clay found in combination with coal seams.

GROUTING OR POINTING The filling between tiles or mosaic tessera, consisting of a hard-setting substance.

GROG Fired clay in the form of biscuitware, ground to varying degrees of fineness, and used to give texture, to reduce shrinkage and to reduce plasticity in a clay body. The refractory quality will vary greatly according to firing temperature and composition of the biscuit.

JIGGER AND JOLLY A machine, or power wheel attachment, with a metal profile that shapes an article against a revolving plaster mould to which an even layer of clay has first been applied.

KIDNEY RUBBER A piece of flat, tapering, kidney-shaped rubber used for smoothing clay when moulding dishes.

MAJOLICA, DELFT, FAIENCE All these names are used technically to describe the painting of ceramic pigments on an opaque white glaze.

OPACIFIER Substance added to a glaze to make it opaque.

PHOSPHOR BRONZE Non-corroding metal used for the mesh of sieves.

SGRAFFITO A means of decoration where a layer of glaze, slip or pigment has been scratched through to show the surface beneath.

SLIP Clay liquified with the addition of water.

TESSERA Pieces of mosaic, made of coloured glass or ceramic and generally flat, and square in shape.

Temperature conversion

If your equipment is calibrated in the fahrenheit rather than the centigrade scale, you can convert the centigrade temperatures given in the instructions by multiplying the temperature given by 9, dividing by 5 and adding 32 degrees.

Conversion factors for weight units

To change milligrammes into grains, multiply the number of milligrammes given in the text by ·0154.

To change grammes into ounces, multiply the number of grammes by ·0353.

To change kilogrammes into pounds, multiply the number of kilogrammes by 2·205.

(1 kilogramme = 1000 grammes; 1 gramme = 1000 milligrammes.)

Index

Where there are several page references, the most important are shown in heavy type.

Index [*continued*]